GLIMPSES

GLIMPSES OF HIS Glory

JOHN AND ELIZABETH SHERRILL

Tyndale House Publishers, Inc., Wheaton, Illinois

Library of Congress Cataloging-in-Publication Data

Sherrill, John L.
    Glimpses of his glory / John and Elizabeth Sherrill.
        p.   cm.
    Essays originally published in Guideposts, 1952-1990.
    ISBN 0-8423-1082-7
    1. Christian life—1960-   2. God.   3. Sherrill, John L.
4. Sherrill, Elizabeth.   I. Sherrill, Elizabeth.   II. Title.
BV4501.2.S43833 1991
242—dc20   91-20486

For material previously published in *Guideposts* magazine and *Daily
Guideposts*, copyright 1952, 1953, 1954, 1955, 1956, 1958, 1959, 1962,
1963, 1964, 1965, 1966, 1967, 1968, 1969, 1970, 1971, 1972, 1976,
1978, 1980, 1982, 1983, 1985, 1986, 1987, 1988, 1989, 1990 by
Guideposts Associates Inc., Carmel, New York 10512.

Original material copyright © 1990 by John and Elizabeth Sherrill. "The
Competitor" originally appeared in *Christian Herald* and is copyright by
John and Elizabeth Sherrill. "The Tradition" originally appeared in
Charisma and *Christian Life* magazine, Lake Mary, FL 32746. Copyright
© 1981 Strang Communications Co.

99 98 97 96 95 94 93 92 91
10 9   8   7   6   5   4   3   2   1

CONTENTS

INTRODUCTION
SEEING GOD

"If God is real," our four-year-old grandson asked not long ago, "why can't I see Him?"

It's a profound question, one that saints and skeptics have asked through the ages. "Show us the Father," Jesus' disciples begged. And "show us the Father" has been our plea through forty years as reporters.

They've been exciting years as people from many walks, young and old, rich and poor, have shared with us their intimate adventures. Over the decades we've been invited deep inside other hearts and minds, lived vicariously many lives. We've become . . . a fisherman on Chesapeake Bay, an actress battling loneliness, a doctor to lepers in Africa, a widower in Oklahoma praying for a wife . . . and from each individual we've learned something of value to us personally.

That's why, when it was suggested that we gather some of these experiences together as a book, we agreed with delight. It would be a chance to track our own spiritual odyssey through the people we've known, to reflect on what their struggles and discoveries have meant to our own growing faith.

We knew the choosing would be hard—how to select a

few dozen episodes from among hundreds! But the result, we thought, would be a portrait gallery of some of the men and women who've lighted the way for us, a first road map of our own faltering pilgrims' progress.

So we began the process of sorting and grouping—in mounting astonishment at what we saw. Here was not a collection of character studies, fascinating though these individuals were. Still less a portrait of ourselves. The likeness emerging from these varied events was . . . God's.

God seen in crisis and God seen in the daily routine. God seen in a cry for help and God seen in the hand stretched out to respond.

They were glimpses—glimpses only—of His presence. Fleeting views of His mercy, His provision, His guidance, seen through the filter of human experience. Perhaps that is the only way He can make Himself intelligible to us, the only way human eyes and hearts can lay hold of Him. As the light of the sun is visible only as reflected from motes of dust in the air, perhaps we can see His glory only in its reflection from our small cares and joys.

Why can't we see God? Maybe, we thought, as we relived these moments, we have.

John & Elizabeth Sherrill
Chappaqua, New York
May, 1990

PART ONE

SEEING GOD FOR OURSELVES

Conversion . . .
Making a decision for Christ . . .
Finding God . . .

Whatever words we use, this is the starting place for all the rest: the moment when faith becomes our own. The moment when we first glimpse His glory.

ICE
Sometimes it's hard to take another person's word.

THE LEAP
John can still point to the place where it happened.

SHARK!
They dragged him onto the beach . . . but it was too late.

CRISIS
When the worst happens, a vague Supreme Being can't help.

THE ENABLER
Her husband's alcoholism dominated her life . . . until the night she left him sprawled on the steps.

THE MAN WHO WAS AFRAID OF WATER
The most famous oceanic voyager of our day started out with a terrible handicap.

THE GLUTTON
Seeing God for ourselves is a lifelong adventure.

There's a limit to what words can convey.

ICE

"Mrs. Shallow—" it was as close as the sixteen-year-old African boy could come to pronouncing the name *Sherrill*—"will you tell us again about winter?"

Fifty pairs of eager eyes focused on mine. We'd finished the geography lesson and now it was Conversation Time in this earth-floored school in Uganda.

Three mornings a week I taught in this mud-walled structure baking beneath the equatorial sun. During the geography lesson weeks before, the subject of seasons had come up. "During winter where I live," I'd told them, "water turns to ice." I'd pointed to Lake Victoria shimmering beyond the banana trees. "Lake water becomes so solid you can stand on it."

From then on there was no other topic for Conversation Time. Over and over the young people asked to hear how rain would come down white and slow, how water became hard. Now, looking over the rows of expectant faces, I realized that these things, for them, had the appeal of a fairy tale. How could I get across the reality of "cold" here on the equator?

Of course! The house John and I were renting had a refrigerator with an ice-cube unit. Next day I wrapped the ice tray in newspaper and hurried with it to school. Handing around the cubes, I saw in the students' faces first shock, then wonder, then the incredulous joy of personal discovery.

It's a little like that when we meet God. When we first come into contact with Him—individually, ourselves. We may have known *about* Him for years, read a lot of books, become extremely well-informed on the subject. Nothing prepares us for that unique, wordless encounter with Reality Himself.

Elizabeth

John's work as a religious reporter had given him a lot of head-knowledge about God. Here's his account of the day when intellectual inquiry became personal encounter . . .

THE LEAP

I still remember that I whistled as I strode up New York's Park Avenue that spring morning in 1959. I stepped through the door of my doctor's office and nodded to his receptionist—an old friend by now. I'd been coming here every month since a cancer operation two years previously, and it was always the same: the doctor's skilled fingers running down my neck, a pat on the back, "See you in a month."

But not that day. This time the fingers prodded and worked a long time. When I left I had an appointment at Memorial Hospital for surgery two days later.

What a difference in a spring morning!

I walked back down the same street in the same sunshine, but now a cold, light-headed fear walked with me. All cancer patients know this fear. We stay on top of it with various mental tricks. Mine was the notion that one operation was all right; it was only if they called you back that you had to worry. Now I could no longer hold the fear down. It rose up, scattering reason before it: this was the Fear of Death.

I dove into the first church I came to, looking for

darkness and privacy more than anything. It was St. Thomas Episcopal on Fifth Avenue. Mechanically, I sat down. A few minutes later, to my surprise, a young minister mounted the pulpit to give a noonday meditation. I didn't know it then, but this brief address was to provide the key which would rid me of this most basic of all fears.

At the time it seemed wretchedly irrelevant to my problem. The young man spoke on Nicodemus. Many of us try, he said, to approach Christ as Nicodemus did: through logic. "But it isn't logic," said the minister, "that lets us know who Jesus is. It's an experience."

At the time, as I say, this meant nothing to me. And yet the very next morning I was to hear these same words again. My wife Tib and I were having coffee after a sleepless night when the phone rang. It was a neighbor, Catherine Marshall LeSourd.

"John," she said, "could you come over for a few minutes? I've heard the news and there's something I've got to say to you."

Catherine met us at the door wearing neither make-up nor a smile, which said more than words about the concern she felt. She led us into the family room and plunged in without polite talk.

"I know this is presumptuous of me. I'm going to talk to you about your religious life, and I have no right to assume that it lacks anything. After all, you and Tib have been writing for *Guideposts* for almost ten years. You've investigated Christianity from many angles. But often those who know most about religion are farthest from the real, life-changing heart of it."

I looked at Tib. She sat still as a rock.

"John," said Catherine, "do you believe Jesus was God?"

It was the last question in the world I expected. I'd supposed she would say something about God being able to heal, or prayer being effective—something to do with my crisis. But since she had put the question to me, I considered it. Tib and I were Christians in the sense that we wrote "Protestant" on application blanks, attended church with some regularity, sent our children to Sunday school. Still, I knew that these were habits. I had never really come to grips with the question, was Jesus of Nazareth, in fact, God?

"You might ask what difference it makes," said Catherine. "It spells the difference between life and death, John. The Bible tells us that when we believe in Christ we no longer have to die, but are given everlasting life."

Yes, but . . . it was precisely over this issue of belief that I always had my difficulty. I knew what the Bible promised, and I admired and envied people who accepted it unquestioningly. For myself, there were roadblocks of reason which invariably halted me. I started to map them for Catherine, but she stopped me.

"You're trying to approach Christ through logic, John," she said. "Faith isn't a philosophical proposition. It's an experience."

There it was again. "It's one of the peculiarities of Christianity," Catherine went on, "that you have to experience it *before* you can understand it. And that's what I'm hoping for you today . . . that without having any of your questions answered, you make the leap of faith—right over all your doubts—to Christ."

There was silence in the room. I had an eternity of reservations and, at the same time, a sudden desire to do exactly what she was suggesting. The biggest reservation I admitted frankly: it didn't seem right to shy away all these years and then come running when I had cancer and was scared. "I'd feel like a hypocrite," I said.

"John," said Catherine, almost in a whisper, "that's pride. You want to come to God in your way. When you will. As you will. Strong and healthy. Maybe God wants you just as you are, without a shred to recommend you."

When we left, I still had not brought myself to take that step. But halfway home, passing a certain telephone pole on Millwood Road in Chappaqua, a pole which I can point out today, I turned suddenly to Tib and said:

"I'm making that leap. I believe that Jesus was God."

That's all I said. Yet I believe now that in some unaccountable way, in that instant, I died.

I didn't think of it in those terms at the time, and yet . . . certainly it wrenched like death. It was a coldblooded laying down of my sense of what was logical, quite without emotional conviction. And with it went something that was essentially "me." All the bundle of self-consciousness that we call our ego somehow seemed involved in this decision.

I was amazed at how much it hurt, how desperately this thing inside me fought for life, so that there was a real kind of slaying required. But when it was dead and quiet finally, and I blurted out my simple statement, there was room in me for something new and altogether mysterious.

The first hint that there was something different about me came next morning at the hospital, when a snappy young nurse came into give me an injection. Since Army days I have had a morbid horror of needles. Yet this time . . .

"All right, over we go," the nurse said crisply. But when she had finished, her tone changed. "My, you're a relaxed one! You act like you're here for a vacation."

It wasn't until after she'd left that I realized how true and how remarkable this was. I *was* relaxed, deeply and truly. It was as if in some secret and undefined part of myself I knew that, no matter how this operation turned out, it was only an inconvenience in an existence that was new and strange and quite independent of hospitals and surgeons, illness and recovery.

Back at home the following week, waiting out the laboratory report, this curious unconcern continued. Without working at it in the least, my attitude was one of a man who had nothing to fear. How was it possible?

Then I had a strange thought: a man who had already died would certainly not be afraid of death. And that was just how I felt—as though death were somehow behind me.

Wondering if there was any biblical backing for this idea, I got out a Bible and concordance. And there it was in the fifth chapter of John:

"In very truth," Christ told His disciples, "anyone who gives heed to what I say, and puts his trust in him who sent me, has hold of eternal life and does not come up for judgment, but already has passed from death to life" (John 5:24, NEB).

How can I describe the excitement that leapt to me from that page? Was it possible that when I took that leap of faith an actual new life began for me, existing parallel to my earthly life but strangely apart from it? A life that was born of the Spirit and was using my perishable body only temporarily?

If so, then I should see evidence of something new inside me—something that owed nothing to my earth-bound existence.

And I did.

The first evidence came when the doctor's report arrived. It was a hopeful one; but I found that this had ceased to be of primary importance to me. Something else seemed far more pressing: to discover what this new life was, where it came from, what it meant.

I had an insatiable hunger to explore the New Testament, which I read with a sense of . . . recognition. Wasn't it likely that this was the new life, recognizing its natural environment of spirit, feeding on a new kind of food which it needed as my body needed physical food?

The same was true of church. Suddenly I couldn't wait for Sunday: churchgoing was no longer a habit, but a necessity.

And—perhaps the most important evidence of all—Christ, whom I had approached as a problem in logic, became for me a living Person. I feel now that it was Jesus I sought and found in the Bible, in the sacraments, and in the company of Christians.

Thirty years have passed now since the day Tib and I drove past that telephone pole on Millwood Road. They've been fabulous years, filled with meaning and adventure and wonder. I found, as time passed and I came down from my mountain top and slipped into old patterns I'd hoped I'd left behind, that the new life continued along its sovereign track, undeterred by the stumblings and meanderings of my earthly walk. It was as if the life which began that day was not dependent on my faithfulness, but on Christ's.

And it is this which gives me the conviction that it is indeed life everlasting . . .

John

How long does it take to step from theorizing about God, into His living presence? This is a story of sudden life on a California beach . . .

SHARK!

Most of the people strolling on Baker's Beach on the afternoon of May 7, 1959, were congratulating each other on having escaped the heat downtown. Two of them, though, were not discussing the unusually hot, bright weather.

Shirley O'Neill and Albert Kogler, freshmen at San Francisco State College, were talking about something else, a strange subject for a May afternoon. How strange Shirley did not know until later. She and Albert were talking about death.

"It's not death that should worry us," she was saying earnestly. "It's loss of God. That's what we're here for, Al—to prepare for eternity!"

They walked silently for a moment, letting their eyes follow the great orange span of the Golden Gate Bridge. Then Al laughed. "Well, I don't have to do my preparing now. I'm not going to die today!"

But, as it turned out, he was wrong.

Shirley and Al had come down for a swim after their last afternoon class. It was funny, Shirley thought, nearly every time she saw Al they seemed to get on the subject

14

of religion. She was Catholic and he was always asking questions. He himself was, as he put it, "not much of anything."

But, thought Shirley, Al was very much something. He was one of these individuals everybody likes instantly, probably because he himself was so full of love for people. He'd said once that he wished there was a world after death where he would meet everybody again.

"But you've never been baptized, Al. I'm not talking just as a Catholic. Baptism is the first thing all Christians do, if they want this love-centered world after death."

"I don't know," he'd always say. "Anyway there's plenty of time to decide things like that."

Now as they walked up the beach, Al looked at his watch. "Hey!" he said. "It's almost five-thirty! If we want that swim we'd better get it!"

The next moment he had run through the surf and disappeared beneath a breaker. With a splash Shirley followed him. The surf was rough and there was a strong undertow. For a minute or two she fought the waves, raising herself between dunkings for a sight of Al's head. Then she was in the calm, deep water fifty yards from shore.

"Hi!" Al was waiting for her. They smiled lazily at each other, treading water. "Beats sitting in the library, doesn't it?"

Shirley nodded, squinting in the glare of the sun. Out in the channel the fishing fleet was heading in from the open ocean. Up the beach two men in hip boots were casting into the surf with long rods.

Suddenly the warm green-and-gold afternoon was split

with a scream. It was an instant before Shirley realized it had come from Al. She whirled round to him. Out of the water rose a great gray shape. It hung there for a moment, then toppled over into the water.

Al's head appeared again. "Get away, Shirley!" he shrieked. "Get away! It's a shark!"

With horror, Shirley watched a stream of blood rise to stain the green water. Get away! The words jarred her into motion. She turned and stroked frantically for the shore. Get away! Behind her she could hear the thrashing of the shark. She was twenty feet away when Al screamed again.

She stopped, her heart hammering in her throat. Then she turned around. Every fiber of her body told her to go the other way, towards land, towards safety. But something stronger still drew her to Al. Ahead of her the water boiled and churned, blood red. Now she could almost touch him. She reached for his arm, then drew back. The arm had been torn from his shoulder.

She swam close and slipped her arm around his chest. "Don't kick, Al! Lie still!"

Lying on her back, stroking with her legs and her free arm, she pulled him slowly—oh so slowly!—toward the shore, every second expecting to feel the teeth of the shark. She was shouting now with Al: "Help! Help us!" But the sunbathers dozed on under the blue sky, the roar of the surf shutting them off from the terror in the sea.

Close legs, stroke, close legs, stroke. Shirley was a strong swimmer, but with each pause the undertow dragged them seaward again. It seemed to her that the shore was no nearer than before, that it would never be any nearer. A wave washed over her face. She gasped and clutched Al tighter. Two minutes later her feet touched bottom. Then a wave broke over them and they both went under. She struggled up, dragging Al's head to the surface, and again was knocked down.

Four times they went down. Then one of the fishermen glanced that way. In an instant, Joe Intersonine was racing down the beach. With a well-aimed cast he dropped the end of his line into the surf beside Shirley. She wrapped it round her waist and hung on as he reeled in.

They dragged Al a few feet up onto the sand, then Shirley dropped on her knees beside him.

"Air!" Al spoke so faintly she could hardly hear him. "Please, air!"

People were running from all over the beach. Someone laid a blanket over him. Crouching lower, Shirley put her mouth over his and blew into his throat. Breath in . . . breath out . . . breath in . . . At last from the cliff above came the wail of an ambulance.

But where Al's arm had been, too much blood had been lost. Now Shirley looked into the brown eyes so close to hers and saw the thing she feared. Already Al seemed a great distance from the beach and her, from this familiar earth.

"Al," she whispered, "let me baptize you! Al, is it all right?"

Gradually the distant eyes focused on hers. "Yes," he said. "Please."

Shirley leapt up and ran to the water. She held her

bathing cap in the surf and let the foaming seawater fill it. Then she ran back to Al and knelt beside him.

"I baptize thee," she said slowly, as the water ran over his forehead, "in the name of the Father, of the Son, and of the Holy Ghost."

The ambulance had reached the top of the cliff. It could not descend the steep path so a Coast Guard crash truck started down.

"Al," Shirley whispered, "say this after me, "Oh my God, I am heartily sorry for having offended Thee . . ."

"Oh my God," Al repeated. His eyes closed. "I am . . . I am . . ."

"If you can't talk, just follow the words," Shirley begged. "Say them in your heart: "I detest all my sins because I dread the loss of heaven and the pains of hell, but most of all because they offend Thee, my God, Who art all good and deserving of all my love . . ."

Men were taking a stretcher from the truck. Al's eyes opened suddenly. "I love God and I love my parents and I love people! Oh God help me, God help me!"

The stretcher bearers lifted the dying young man into the truck. All around people were talking in hushed voices. "It would take a miracle to save him," a woman said.

Shirley sank to the ground. "We'd better get her to the hospital too," a Coast Guardsman said. She felt strong arms around her, lifting her. Dazed and weary as she was, she was sure of one thing. Shirley O'Neill knew that the miracle for Al had already happened.

Elizabeth

As a scientist, he acknowledged the existence of a Supreme Being. But when his son was murdered, William Blankenship found that an impersonal God is not enough . . .

CRISIS

Saturday night, April 30, 1955. At 8:45 P.M., a fifteen-year-old high school student named Billy Blankenship got his parents' permission to walk to a neighborhood movie house with a friend. Billy raced down the stairs from his family's fourth-floor apartment at 3454 Fenton Avenue, the Bronx, New York, joined his friend, Salvatore Siciliano, outside the building, and the two boys set out.

Ten minutes later Billy Blankenship was shot to death.

Billy and Salvatore were crossing a vacant lot lined with weeds, broken glass and heaven trees, when five boys rode up on bicycles. The five boys wore black leather jackets trimmed in yellow. There were pictures of Indians on the jackets, signifying their membership in a street gang known as the Navajos. The Navajos stopped Billy and Salvatore.

"What are you doing in this neighborhood?" one of the boys asked Billy. Billy didn't understand. He was in his own neighborhood.

"I don't know what you mean."

"You're a member of the Golden Guineas!" The Guineas were another street gang, rivals of the Navajos.

"No, I'm not," Billy said, still mystified.

"Come here!"

The five boys dragged Billy to the back of the lot, asked more questions. One of the boys pulled out a .32 caliber Beretta. The boy held the gun against Billy's left arm and pulled the trigger. The bullet passed through Billy's arm and hit his heart. As the five boys fled, Salvatore ran to telephone the police. While he was gone, Billy Blankenship died among the weeds and broken glass and heaven trees.

This is the story of the four days that followed. During these four days, there were two funerals for Billy, one there in the Bronx, the second in the town of Tamaqua, Pennsylvania, where Billy was born. And during those four days, Billy's father faced a crisis. He felt totally alone, unable to get help from his wife, Helen, because she was as much in need of comfort as he was; unable to get help from his friends, because none of his friends had had a son murdered and could not know what his grief was like; unable to get help from his religion, because he did not believe in the kind of a God who could reach down and show personal concern for individuals.

At first, William Blankenship simply found no help at all.

By the third night after the murder, he had very nearly cracked under the strain. On that night the maroon-walled apartment on Fenton Avenue, number 4-D, was full of people. For three days they had been coming.

At eleven o'clock Blankenship sank down on the sofa. He was a large man: six feet three inches, 220 pounds. His outstretched arms extended past the back of the sofa on both sides.

"Please, no more visitors, Milton."

Milton Visnic, a young cop from a nearby apartment, was Blankenship's closest friend. Visnic nodded, escorted the remaining callers to the door and locked it. Helen Blankenship went into the bedroom to try to get some sleep. Her husband followed to say good night, returned, sat down again. There was along silence.

"How far is it to Tamaqua?" Visnic said at last. Visnic had agreed to drive down next day with the family.

"Four hours," Blankenship said.

"Do you want me to stay the night, Bill?"

Blankenship shook his head. "Go get some sleep. It'll be a long day." He got off the sofa and went to the door with his friend. And then he was alone.

He sat down on the sofa again and let his mind wander back to his secure, younger days in North Carolina, where he'd graduated from the University at Chapel Hill. He had wanted to be a teacher. But he couldn't support a family teaching, so he went into industry instead, becoming a research chemist with the International Latex Corporation. But he never lost his desire to teach.

All around him in the maroon living room was the proof: books. Every time one of his sons showed a spark of interest in a new field, William Blankenship bought all the books he could find on the subject. Then in the evening, he had the boys read aloud, taking turns. First Doug, who was seventeen, then Billy, fifteen, then Randy, eleven. Gary, who was six, just listened.

One time Billy expressed an interest in boats. Blankenship went downtown and bought dozens of official navigation charts, a book of logarithms, manuals on sailing, and spread them out on the floor. The four boys and their father sailed around the world—on the living room rug. Billy had a favorite moorage in the Bahamas. It was a tip of land named Billy's Point.

There were books on sex and automobile mechanics and music. But with it all, the Blankenship boys were no bookworms. Billy was a good football player, popular at neighborhood dances. All this pleased William Blankenship. By spending a lot of time with his boys, he thought he was doing his best to combat juvenile delinquency.

But that was not all he had done. He was president of a local citizens' group, the Bronxdale Civic League, that organized hundreds of fathers to clean up vacant lots for ball fields. He helped organize community dances, saw that they were properly supervised. He fought for and got better lights on the dark side streets.

William Blankenship also believed that young people need a solid ethical orientation based on religion. He often took his family to the Presbyterian Church near the lot where Billy was killed. But he felt religion was best taught at home.

So he bought books on religion.

The Blankenships started with primitive religions and mythology and went on to the great religions of the world. Here in this room the Blankenships had read aloud from the Torah and the Koran, read and analyzed the Bible from cover to cover. With his training in science, William Blankenship tried to be objective about his religion. He believed in God—as a First Cause, the creative force which set the universe in motion and established its immutable laws.

Thinking back over the discussions in this room, William Blankenship realized that night that his own religion had not been much help to him these past three days. What good did it do to know statistics about the various faiths when . . . when there was no help in statistics. William Blankenship was a strong, vigorous man. But that night he cried.

The funeral chapel at Tamaqua is made of gray fieldstone. It was crowded with friends of the Blankenships who had come as an expression of their shared grief.

William and Helen Blankenship were standing alone outside the chapel before the service: they were supposed to enter last of all. Suddenly Helen Blankenship spoke. "I can't," she said. She looked at her husband and finished the sentence with her eyes.

They had reached the end. They could not go to this second funeral of their son. They waited to see if they could pull themselves together for the sake of their other boys. No strength came to them. No help.

Then, in his desperation, William Blankenship did what for him was a strange thing, out of character. There, outside the chapel, he got down on his knees. It had been years since William Blankenship had been on his knees. But that morning in the blue hills of Pennsylvania, he took Helen's hand and together they knelt. Together they said a simple prayer. It seemed to them that the same words came to their lips almost simultaneously. While they knelt, help, at last, did come, and shortly after, they arose and went in to kneel at Billy's bier.

For a long time William Blankenship refused to talk about that prayer. But eventually he did. Because in that moment he found a God who was more than an impersonal, creative force. In that moment, William Blankenship found a God who could give help to individuals in time of trouble.

As William and Helen Blankenship knelt, they said, "God, there's such a thing as a grief no human being can help." They were silent a while, then continued. "But You can help," they said. "You understand. Your son was murdered too."

John

Seeing God for ourselves . . . there are two parties to this equation: God and the "self" who seeks the relationship. Here's how one woman discovered that selflessness is not always a virtue . . .

THE ENABLER

"God first. Others second. Myself last." For the last forty years a group of people have been challenging this seemingly admirable order. They're the sister group to Alcoholics Anonymous, *Al-Anon,* which focuses not on the problem drinker himself, but on the wife, husband, child, parent, friend—anyone who must live with an alcoholic.

Sylvia B. is typical in many ways of the people for whom Al-Anon exists. Her husband had been a problem drinker for eleven years. For five of them Sylvia did not buy a single new dress. Bob was too expensive. She paid damages twice to keep him out of jail (one smashed window, one wrecked car). To keep him out of the state hospital, she took a job and sent him to private doctors.

Every time he sobered up, Bob thanked Sylvia with tears of gratitude. He would promise her the world and she would buy him a new suit of clothes. Sometimes he hocked the suit that week, sometimes not for a month or more. Then she would resume her nightly patrol of park benches. Home by cab: "He's not feeling well, driver."

(Hoping it wasn't the same one as last week.) Up the front steps (twelve of them). Clean up the mess. Beg. Reproach. Threaten. Her whole life was devoted to Bob's drinking.

The fact that she herself needed help with the hard job of being an alcoholic's spouse never occurred to Sylvia. But then one night when she was asking an AA friend once more to talk to Bob, the friend interrupted gently:

"Sylvia, neither you nor I nor anybody else can talk to Bob till he wants to listen." He went on before she could speak. "At our last AA meeting we had a speaker from Al-Anon . . ."

Sylvia hardly heard the rest. A new group! To her that meant one thing: *this* group, *this* time, might have the secret of changing Bob.

When she walked into the basement room of the church where the Al-Anon meeting was in progress, seven women, three men and a teen-age boy were deep in conversation around a large table. They introduced themselves to her, using first names only, and resumed their discussion. One by one, around the table, they talked about the subject for the evening. This week it was prayer: how they prayed, what benefits they discovered, what the stumbling blocks were.

For nearly an hour Sylvia listened in astonishment. No one talked about how to make an alcoholic stop drinking. Alcohol was never mentioned. These people were not discussing someone else's problems, they were discussing their own!

After an hour everyone stood up and two of the women

began passing coffee and cake. A white-haired lady came up to Sylvia.

"I know it's confusing the first time you come," she said. "We're working on the Twelve Steps of AA, you see. We're on the eleventh step now—that's the one when we try to get close to God through prayer."

"I know all about the Twelve Steps!" Sylvia protested. "I've tried over and over to get my husband to follow them. But they're for alcoholics, not for us!"

The older woman put a gentle hand on Sylvia's arm. "Believe me, my dear, we need them as badly as they do." And over coffee, she told Sylvia the story of Al-Anon.

Nobody really knows when Al-Anon began or who started it. By the mid-1940s little groups of men and women were already meeting in different parts of the country to address a common need. These people had discovered that years of living with an alcoholic had left scars on their own personalities—some so deep that they remained even if the drinking ceased. If alcoholics could find help by banding together in AA, perhaps their families could benefit from a support group too.

Soon the scattered family groups began to correspond. By the time I met Sylvia in 1958 there were more than a thousand groups representing every state in the union and twenty foreign countries. Since then its numbers have doubled each decade. But for all its growth, Al-Anon has never become a "big" organization. It has no president, no rules, no dues, no set pattern for meetings. It remains what it started out to be: men and women getting together because they themselves need help.

And they find it, as Sylvia discovered to her amazement, the same way alcoholics do: through the Twelve Steps of AA. The first step says,

> *We admitted we were powerless over alcohol—that our lives had become unmanageable.*

For the alcoholic, this realization is essential to everything that follows; without it he cannot be helped.

But in a special way it is also the essential first step for the alcoholic's family. Like Sylvia, most people who love an alcoholic believe that *they* can somehow induce him to stop drinking. They try pouring his liquor down the sink. Warning local bars not to serve him. Rationing his money. Pleading. Bargaining. With involvement in Al-Anon, all such activity ceases.

The second step is equally important:

> *We came to believe that a Power greater than ourselves could restore us to sanity.*

"Let Go and Let God," is the profound wisdom learned at Al-Anon. The last ten steps are a spiritual journey out of self-pity, self-righteousness—whatever one's individual shortcomings—toward a personal knowledge of God.

To know whether a spiritual approach to such a problem works, you have only to drop in on an Al-Anon meeting, as I did with Sylvia. You have to hear the laughter, feel the sympathy, see the love in action—and reflect that each one of these people has had tragedy in his family.

But no longer are they facing it alone. Here is a roomful of people who've been through it all. "So many of us, right in this town!" is the typical reaction. People begin to hold up their heads again. After a few meetings women often give a little extra attention to their hair; men shine up their shoes. One woman who ate candy whenever her husband was on a spree took off thirty pounds in her first five months in Al-Anon.

"I not only look like a human being again," she told me, "but I'm so weak from dieting I don't have the strength to nag at John and he's started staying home."

Time and again after a husband or wife joins Al-Anon, his alcoholic partner joins AA and stops drinking for good. This is not the purpose of Al-Anon. But it is so often a result that there seems to be only one way to explain it. The addictive personality—the same is true of compulsive gamblers, overeaters, drug addicts and many others—will often lean his whole weight on any support that is offered. When that support is withdrawn he may find that he can stand alone. The Al-Anon member learns to stop being an "enabler" of his partner's self-destructive patterns. To let the other person confront his situation without the buffer of a well-meaning intermediary. And this can be the shock that starts him on the road to sobriety.

It worked that way for Sylvia. She left that first meeting feeling a little hurt. She'd come to discuss Bob's problem; instead, people suggested she work on hers. Like many newcomers to Al-Anon, she couldn't see much to criticize in her own behavior—she might not be perfect, but she'd kept things running, hadn't she?

But as weeks passed and she continued attending the sessions, she began to wonder—was it possible she ran things too well? She asked Bob to face facts and then she faced them for him.

The great moment came on a warm spring evening about four months after that first meeting. Sylvia came home late from an Al-Anon session to find Bob asleep on the front steps. He had a door key in his hand, but hadn't gotten it and the keyhole together. Sylvia stood for a moment, staring down at the man she'd loved and married and promised to cherish forever. Then she took out her own key, stepped over her husband and let herself in.

"I went to bed," she told me. "Slept fine, too."

The next morning as she was getting breakfast, Bob walked into the kitchen. "What time did you get in?" he demanded.

"About 11:30."

"Where was I?"

"Sleeping on the steps."

Bob blinked as though he were trying to understand a foreign language. "Why didn't you pick me up?"

Sylvia poured him a cup of coffee, looked him in the eye and said, "Because I didn't put you down."

For Bob, the shock of losing a support he had so long counted on was the beginning of a new life. Within six months he was in AA and despite some brief relapses into old patterns, eventually stopped drinking altogether. The point Sylvia stresses, however, is that even before Bob found his own solution, she had found something beyond price in Al-Anon.

"It's not that I didn't believe in God before," she says. "I prayed all the time."

But she had prayed mainly that God would heal Bob's addiction. "I was so busy asking God to change Bob that I never heard what He wanted changed in me."

In fact, Sylvia had no relationship of her own with God at all. Adoration . . . praise . . . personal repentance . . . prayers for guidance . . . the simple enjoyment of His company—all were overlooked in her single-minded absorption with her husband's problem. "It sounds selfish, but if we don't bring ourselves to God first—for healing, for strength, for growth—then He can't use us to help anyone else."

When did Sylvia's faith become real? When she stepped out from behind her husband's needs and said:

"God, this is Sylvia."

Elizabeth

THE MAN WHO WAS
AFRAID OF WATER

*Thor Heyerdahl was waiting for us outside his hilltop Italian
home overlooking the Mediterranean. Tan and slender, he looked
far younger than his fifty-nine years. "What a beautiful setting,"
we said, "for someone who has always loved the sea."*

*"Loved it?" He gazed out over the blue-green water. "As a
matter of fact, I used to hate the sea—hated and feared it. I had
a terror of all water."*

*A strange statement from someone who had crossed the vast
Pacific on a raft! For more than three months he and his companions
on the* Kon-Tiki *had drifted on mid-ocean currents to demonstrate
his theory that early South Americans could have reached Polynesia.
In all this time they'd seen no land at all, only giant waves towering
over their heads, crashing over the hand-lashed logs . . .*

*He invited us into the cool white walled house—and this is the
story he told.*

As a little boy growing up in Norway, I could see ships
coming and going in the Oslo fjord from the window of
my home. I used to dream of traveling in them to the

faraway places in the pictures in my parents' books, especially two huge volumes almost too big for me to lift down from the shelf: *The Living Races of Mankind.*

As I grew older, my parents, especially my mother, encouraged these interests. Mother was an outstanding natural historian with great respect for whatever could be weighed, measured and researched—and an equal contempt for prayer, superstition, and other "religious nonsense."

My father, on the other hand, was convinced of the existence of a world that could not be seen or touched. In their frequent arguments on the subject, Mother seemed to have all the logic on her side, and yet I could not help noticing that Father had a secret inner joy. He taught me to say the Lord's Prayer and often, at night, after Mother had put me to bed, he would tiptoe into my room to hear me recite it in whispers.

I was still very young when the first water accident happened. In back of our house was a small lake where in winter men used to cut great blocks of ice. One day some bigger boys and I were sliding on this frozen lake when we began daring each other to jump onto one of the blocks.

As the one who weighed least, I was elected to try it first. The great ice block wobbled under me, then capsized with a splash. Suddenly I was in a frigid, swirling, utterly confusing world. I thrashed wildly in all directions. Which way was the surface? I was unconscious when they hauled me out.

A few years later I had a second near-drowning. I had

started school by now and had gone with a group of classmates on a swimming party. I did not go in the water—I refused even to try to learn to swim—but sat on the bank watching the others.

At last they came out and, to dry off, started a game of tag. We chased each other higher and higher up the steep banks of the fjord. At one point a narrow footbridge led across a deep tidal inlet onto a small island. I started across it with my pursuer at my heels. I scrambled over the edge, leaped for the shore—and plunged straight into the churning water far below. I heard the screams of my schoolmates high above me as I rose to the surface, only to be dragged beneath again. The third time the deadly clutch released me, someone had thrown me a life preserver.

We interrupted Mr. Heyerdahl. "These experiences must have made the question of life after death very real and personal."

Heyerdahl nodded. He'd wanted to have his father's joyful certainty about God, yet at the same time felt himself increasingly committed to his mother's concern for the provable. Standing in the way of those early dreams of travel and discovery, however, was his paralyzing fear of water.

My father tried for years to help me get over my fear, arguing that it was far more dangerous to avoid water than to learn to swim. He even tried bribery—a five-kroner note if I would go into the water up to my chest, ten kroners if I put my head under—but I couldn't do it. For a time he hired a professional swimming instructor who buckled me into a harness suspended from a pole by a rope. But if the rope at my back slackened even a little, panic swept over me and I clawed wildly at the surface. Defeated, my father gave up the lessons.

More years went by in which I was developing the controversial theory of westward migration by raft to the Polynesian islands. All the experts said no one could sail the open ocean in a raft. I wanted to test my theory by actually floating across the Pacific on the Humboldt Current, as I was certain early seafarers had done. But how to overcome my crippling fear of water?

As it turned out, World War II forced me to abandon such speculations for a while. And it was a wartime incident that made me face up to my fear.

I happened to be in Canada when the Nazis invaded Norway. I joined the Free Norwegian Forces in Ontario, preparing troops for guerrilla warfare in our occupied country.

In wartime, private fears and phobias are not things you admit to, and so one day I found myself on a portage trip with two other Norwegian soldiers on the wild Oxtongue River. It was early spring and the river was rampaging with melting glacial water; we had to portage our canoe around innumerable rapids and falls. At last we reached the foot of High Falls, a vast cataract thundering over the crest of a precipice far above us. We wrestled the heavy canoe up the trail and along the portage path above the falls.

There to our dismay, not fifty yards from the brink of the cataract, the path vanished beneath the spring flood waters: the sheer rock cliff plunged directly into the river.

Just against the cliff the water seemed calmer, forming

little eddies and backwaters against the furious cresting of the center. Perhaps by sitting in the canoe and clutching roots and cracks in the cliff face we could haul ourselves upstream far enough to begin paddling.

For two hundred yards the stratagem worked. The deafening roar of the falls receded a bit. And then just ahead, the cliff jutted sharply out into the stream. We were inching our way, hand over hand, around this promontory when a side current caught the bow.

In one awful second I knew we were going over.

Then I was tumbling in the very center of the foaming torrent. When my head finally broke water, I saw the capsized canoe racing toward the falls and one of my companions clinging to the rocky shore. Then my heavy winter uniform and thick army boots dragged me again beneath the surface.

Incredibly, even as I felt myself swept toward the precipice, I had a clear, almost dispassionate thought: in a moment I will know beyond all doubt which of my parents is right about life after death. With that thought came a memory . . . my father tiptoeing into my room at night. With the boom of the cataract sounding closer each second, I started to pray.

As I did, I felt a sudden burst of will. I would fight. I would not yield. As my prayer grew surer, warmth seemed to flood my frozen body. I struggled to the surface and began to swim with long, strong strokes, my feet in their waterlogged boots beating out a rhythmic kicking. As I continued to swim—I who couldn't swim—the warmth turned into a kind of joy, the certainty that something greater than myself had reached down inside me.

There was no doubt about it, the cliff face was slipping away less quickly now; I was almost keeping pace with the racing water. Each time I thought I must stop, that I could not go on, the strange joy reappeared and I struggled on, helped by nothing I could see or describe.

Now I saw that both my buddies were safe. One of them was holding on to a tree limb, leaning out over the water toward me. Though exhausted, I fought on against the current. My companion was stretching out his hand. I battled the last few inches. Finally I felt his fingertips.

And that is how, years later, after the war, I was able to set out on the *Kon-Tiki* across the Pacific. I had learned for myself what my father had always known, that there is an invisible world of caring around and within us—different from the visible world, unmeasurable by physical tools, but as provable as the fact of life, as close as a cry from the heart.

John and Elizabeth

Five years after his "leap of faith," John learns that making faith personal is a process that never ends.

THE GLUTTON

For a while after I became a Christian, I believed that my life had been totally changed. The Bible itself encouraged me in this. "If any man be in Christ," wrote Paul, "he is a new creature: old things are passed away; behold, all things are become new" (2 Corinthians 5:17, KJV).

Yet as time passed I found many old and destructive patterns still with me. And all around me I observed that this is too often the case with Christians. I knew one faithful churchgoer who hated Jews. Another had a ridiculous sense of his own importance. A minister I knew felt a deep antipathy for his own son. Even those closest to Christ felt the sting of the enigma: James and John vied for honors in heaven; the Christians at Corinth slid from glorifying God into debauchery.

Are we all hypocrites, then, who say we are Christians, yet lead imperfect lives? Don't we know from experience that in many areas we are frustratingly the same after conversion as before?

Shortly after I began grappling with this problem in Christian living, I met a dynamic minister who has arrived at what, for me at any rate, is a valid understanding of this seeming contradiction. This man, a Southerner by the inheritance of generations, felt that as a Christian he must take a positive stand in the then-current civil rights struggle. He, therefore, continued to send his son to his newly integrated school, although it was being boycotted by most of the rest of the white community.

He acted this way, as I say, because of his Christian convictions. But ironically, some of the angriest criticism of him came from members of his own church. These were the people I wanted to know about: "What do you make of their Christianity?" I asked. His answer has stuck with me.

"It is my feeling," he said, "that we appropriate our conversion in different areas at different rates. Many of my parishioners have simply not yet matured into Christ's view of brotherhood. But I do not question the genuineness of their conversion, nor its effectiveness on other levels."

Now, I don't know what the theological status of this idea is; I only know it describes something that I see. It is as though Christ transforms those areas of our lives which we surrender to Him, but will not force from us what we do not freely give.

It has been so in my own life. I did experience a total conversion to the knowledge that God came down to earth in the form of a human being. In this area—the starting point, the essential one—I am truly in Christ, as Paul says, and here it is clear to me that I am a new creature.

But if I expected to find the habits and attitudes of a

lifetime swept away and a new and Christlike character substituted for the one I had been feeding through the years, I was due to be sadly disappointed. And I believe now that Christ rarely works in this way. Conversion seems to be an ongoing process as much as a status.

So how do we get on with this growth process, we infant Christians? I decided to pick some recalcitrant area of my own behavior for an experiment in pinpoint appropriation of my re-birthright.

Before choosing, I set up some ground rules. I would select, I decided, some attitude or habit or preoccupation which consumed time and energy that properly belonged to God or to other people.

Next, I'd face up to my helplessness in the grip of this sin. By myself I could not beat it. I could only confess that this was so, and ask God to accomplish what I could not.

Then from what I knew of the pattern of any conversion, I would have to take some public step, parallel to going forward to the altar at a Billy Graham revival, or kneeling before the bishop for confirmation. Some action which would serve to commit me in the sight of at least one other person to the transformation I was claiming.

And after that I felt I should relax. My effort would no longer be the negative one of trying to combat a failing; it would be the positive one of keeping my attention centered expectantly on Him.

The area that I finally settled on for my own experiment was a destructive and time-consuming preoccupation with money. For some people this is a minor vice. Not for me. It was as much of an obsession as pornography or a thirst for revenge can be for other men. It got in the way of relations with other people by occupying the front of my mind even when I was away from my checkbook. And, of course, every minute that we spend being anxious about money or anything else is a moment spent in isolation, separated from God.

Serious as I knew my exessive concern for money to be, however, as I began to pray to see my conversion "realized" in this area, I perceived that it was only a symptom of a far more pervasive malady. I once heard a psychiatrist say that he was surprised at how many of his patients' troubles were traceable to the traditional "root sins": pride, gluttony, sloth, covetousness, anger, lust and envy. Behind my money-fixation I began to see the evil figure not of covetousness, as I might have expected, but of gluttony.

It came as a surprise. Me, a glutton? But as soon as the insight was granted I could see the sprouts from this root sin everywhere. I tended to overdo in a dozen areas, not to taste life but to gulp it. In some areas, such as work, I even tried to make gluttony a virtue. To ask for the conversion of a single area—my relationship to money—might prove to involve more than I had counted on.

But eventually, on a certain afternoon, in the presence of two friends, I did take the step of confessing that I believed Christ to be Lord over the financial side of my life too. One year has passed since that afternoon. What at first I believed to be a single weakness has continued to show new faces. Almost daily now I recognize some varied growth of the hungry, insatiable root below. It will take many more months, perhaps, to recognize all the damage done in my life by the sin of gluttony.

Yet this is not the whole story. For along with horror at its size and destructiveness, I also sense a healing going on deep in my being. Like most healing, it is slow. I still have episodes of unrestrained gluttony. But they are rarer. More frequent are days and even weeks together when to sip, taste and savor is my pleasure.

I don't know why it has taken me so long to see that this new creature the Bible promises, like all creatures, has a growth process. If a person is in Christ all things are indeed new. But all things are not perfected, all at once. We limit His transforming life in us by sealing off areas of ourselves that seem too dear, too dangerous or even too trivial to give up. The process of opening these closed doors is a slow and often painful one.

But the same Lord who first called us to Himself will help us with these subsequent surrenders too. "He who began a good work in you will carry it on to completion until the day of Christ Jesus" (Philippians 1:6, NIV). When that day will be, when Christ is completed in me, God alone knows. But that He is doing it, makes the waiting a grand adventure.

John

PART TWO

SEEING GOD
IN THE
COMMONPLACE

Seeing God in the daily round, as
  well as the exceptional . . .
In the small as well as the
  immense . . .
Listening for His whispers as well
  as His trumpet blasts . . .
Seeing God can happen as
  suddenly as opening our eyes . . .

The Last Sunny Day
The weather was unusually clear, that autumn when we met.

Wall Man
Mr. Rossi gave us more than a solid wall.

A Day on the Bay
What draws them out on the Chesapeake, father and son, generation after generation?

Mrs. Shallow Goes to School
Tib was the teacher in that mud-walled African school. Or was she the one who needed to learn?

Divine Interruptions
Sometimes a detour is the straightest path.

Sauerkraut!
Every time we eat it, we remember the cabbage farmer we met in France.

A Gift Named Molly
It wasn't until she was dying that this young woman learned to live.

The Joy of Doing with Less*
Malcolm Muggeridge could have any life-style he desired. Why did he choose to live so simply?

*Original for this book

SECRETS OF SIMPLICITY
Seeing more of God in the commonplace.

We skipped a lot of classes, but we learned a lot.

THE LAST SUNNY DAY

John is from Kentucky, I'm from New York. We met in 1947 enroute to Europe aboard the *Queen Elizabeth*—discovering with surprise that we were both headed for the University of Geneva in Switzerland. And that, five years apart in age, we were both college juniors; John had served those years in the army during World War II.

But the biggest surprise that fall was the weather. We had been warned that Geneva would be cold and rainy. It was with an air of urgency, therefore, that John peddled his bicycle one bright Tuesday morning to the *pension* where I was boarding.

"This is the last sunny day we'll have," he predicted. "We can make up European History, but we won't get another chance for a picnic."

We missed a lot of European History that term, as one cloudless day followed another, but we got to know Alpine villages and ruined castles—and each other. "It's the last sunny day!" John would call up to my window as he balanced his bike at the curb.

We were married three months after that first impromptu picnic. Today, more than forty years later, we still pause once in a while to enjoy "the last sunny day."

47

It's a family phrase now, and it means more than the weather. It means, "Just for today, let's forget deadlines and unanswered mail and getting clothes to the cleaner's: life is too amazing to be lived always by the clock and the calendar." And we'll take off, to the seashore, or an old friend's, or a walk in the woods.

We know, now, that it isn't really our last opportunity to do these things. We know more about God than we did forty years ago; we know His riches are inexhaustible and ever-renewed. But we know too that in the midst of His boundless provision, we need to take time out to notice . . .

Elizabeth

Perhaps only the great saints learn to see God in everything.
But all around us are people who point the way . . .

WALL MAN

The first hint I had that Antonio Rossi was an unusual man came the day the rocks were delivered. The mammoth dump truck came hissing and grunting down our driveway in Chappaqua, New York, to drop six yards of fieldstone which seventy-four-year-old Mr. Rossi was supposed to use to repair a retaining wall in our backyard.

I was alarmed at the size of the stones. Some were as large as my daughter's tricycle which stood there in the drive. I put through a call to warn Mr. Rossi that the wrong kind of stone had been delivered. I got his married daughter, Sophia, on the line.

"These are young boulders," I said. "They're much too big for a man your father's age to handle."

"Wait there," said Sophia. "I'll bring Dad right over."

In a few minutes Sophia and old Mr. Rossi drove up. Sophia was beaming. "Watch," was all she said.

The frail-looking little man seemed aware that he was on stage. He hitched up his trousers, tottered over to the rock pile, singled out the largest of the stones and rolled it free. He got his wheelbarrow from the car, laid it on its side so that the lip was just under the edge of the stone, then began to rock the boulder back and forth until suddenly, as if by sleight of hand, it was carried up by the wheelbarrow and set safely in the middle of the drive. Mr. Rossi wasn't even red in the face.

Sophia could hardly contain her admiration as her bantam-sized father strode off across the lawn wheeling his rock. She got back into her car. "My dad," she said, "will give you a wall to be proud of."

I hoped she was right. This wall supported the terrace on which our house rested, and every time I looked at the shoddy way it had been built originally, I got angry. Mr. Rossi saw the poor workmanship too. He stood below the wall now, examining the two-inch cracks that had appeared in eight places. "The man who build this wall, he was no stone mason," said Mr. Rossi.

He picked up his sledge hammer and began to knock down a part of the disgraceful wall, bursting into song as he did so. When he saw that I was still there he turned around and let his joy beam on me for a moment. "I'm a wall man!" he said. "When I fix him up you can forget about him."

Certainly if steadiness of work were the yardstick, Mr. Rossi meant to give me a great wall. He arrived each morning at eight and left after six, and the only break he took in that ten-hour day was the twenty minutes it took him to eat lunch. My office is in my home. I found myself waiting eagerly each day for twelve o'clock to arrive so that I could take a sandwich out and join him. Mr. Rossi's menu never varied—one chunk of Italian bread, one orange, one thermos of coffee.

During our lunches, Mr. Rossi told me in a hundred ways how much he enjoyed his work. It had been a great day, he said, when he turned seven and was apprenticed to a stone mason in Sicily. The only dark hour in his career had come when he arrived in America over fifty years ago and had to work in a rock quarry for twelve cents an hour.

"That's bad," I agreed. "Twelve cents isn't much."

"Twelve cents was enough!" said Mr. Rossi. "What was bad—it was not walls!"

Within a few months, however, Mr. Rossi had returned to his trade. He spent the next half century building monuments to his art: the local school, churches, bridges, gardens, walls of every description.

I have never known a man to use "God" more frequently in his conversation. "True in God, I build you a good wall now," he said again and again. "Si. If God wills, I'll be here Saturday." "No. It will not rain. God, He's watching over my wall."

Almost always, when he referred to God, he would cross his arms on his chest and roll his blue eyes heavenward. When he addressed God directly, as an added gesture he would tip his hat. One day I asked about his wife, who had been in the hospital. Mr. Rossi's right hand immediately went to his heart; his eyes looked skyward; he took off his hat. "Thank you, God," he said. Only then did he answer: "My wife, she's better."

This respectful tipping of the hat came, for me, to epitomize the strength of Antonio Rossi. For respect was the hallmark of everything he did, whether addressing God or working in stone or dealing with people.

One day the garbage man arrived, saw Mr. Rossi, and the two fell into each other's arms, Italian style. Mr. Rossi had once worked with this man on a construction job and called him "my boy." I could have thought they were indeed father and son, except that the younger man was black.

"I liked working with Pop," he told me. "He always made me feel proud of the job."

"True in God," said Mr. Rossi, "you should feel proud. You are one fine boy of mine."

But the place where Mr. Rossi's respect showed most clearly was in his work. He was a wall man, but he never let his passion for his own particular craft blind him to the innate worth of other things. One day I noticed a slightly irregular interval between two of the great supporting buttresses he was erecting. Then I saw the reason: a slender dogwood tree rose from the spot where the second buttress should have gone. Rather than cut it down, he had redesigned his master work. Another day, he found a scrubby little iris growing at the foot of the wall. He dropped his building rocks three feet from where he needed them, dug his footing awkwardly from the left side rather than the right, and saved the flower. That plant will always have a halo around it for me, because Mr. Rossi saw one there.

I came out to lunch one noon to find him shaking his head over a portion of the wall he had just knocked down. "Stone workers nowadays!" he said sadly. "You make a mistake and you cover him up!" He pointed to a cavity in the wall that had not been properly filled in with cement. Each winter water would settle there, freeze, and crack the wall further.

My response to such discoveries had always been indignation. Because the job had not been done right the first time, I was saddled with an expensive rebuilding job today. But Mr. Rossi wasn't concerned about my budget. It was the original builder he was worried for.

"Poverillo," said Mr. Rossi. "I don't curse him. I ask God to bless him. Think what that work do to him here." He put his hand over his heart. Then he took his hat off and added, "You will bless him, God?"

I am sure that I shall never again see poor workmanship without remembering that prayer.

Nor shall I see good work without remembering Mr. Rossi. He was at our house just three weeks, but in that time he helped me see God in places I had never looked for Him before. On the last day Sophia came to help her father put his mixing trough and hammer, his mason's hoe and wheelbarrow back in the car. Mr. Rossi's work was finished. He stood on top of his wall, taking one last look at a job he had undertaken and completed to his satisfaction. It wove around the dogwood and the iris; it was solid in the parts that didn't show as well as those that did.

"True in God," said Mr. Rossi, "you've got a wall. I give him my life-a-time guarantee."

I watched the seventy-four-year-old man step off—a little cautiously, a little slowly—toward his daughter waiting for him in the car. It was only later that I realized I had not even smiled at his "life-a-time guarantee." It is, no doubt, the best guarantee I shall ever receive.

John

The secret of seeing God is to look for Him in the
minute-by-minute routines of daily life . . .

A DAY ON THE BAY

Leon Lewis tells his story to John

As I steer my fishing boat out of Tyler's Cove into Chesapeake Bay this early morning, I glance back through the wheelhouse window. There in the stern of the *Agnes Elizabeth* is my son Lemuel, thirty-five now, sitting on an upended bushel basket sharpening his knife. Standing near him is his son Stephen, eleven and raw boned like his dad. Stephen is out with us for just the day; he's peering through the mist now to see the sun come up over the Maryland shore.

Three generations of Lewises on board. And nobody knows how many Lewis fathers and sons before us have worked here on the bay, oystering and crabbing and fishing, since the family came over from England three hundred years ago.

As I clear the cove, heading for our nets an hour away, young Stephen appears at the wheelhouse door, not saying anything, just waiting, as his father and his uncles waited when they were eleven years old.

"All right, Steve," I say, "take the wheel."

Steve must have had his basket ready on the deck just outside. In no time he has it upside down behind the wheel and is standing on it scanning the water ahead. I don't have to tell him to keep the red channel markers to port. I wave to a crabber, out checking his pots. With Steve at the wheel the boat plows steadily along and I settle back . . .

Some people might wonder why we Lewises keep coming onto the water. Why do we get up at four in the morning, knowing we might not get back until eleven at night? Why do we put up with uncertainty, never knowing what the catch will be or what the market will bring? And the danger. The Chesapeake can be as violent as it is beautiful. One of my brothers was drowned here; I've had a boat sink under me; and out there to port I can see where our firstborn, Bud, Lemuel's older brother, went down when he was just twenty years old.

But here we are, more than two decades later, Lem and Steve and I, out on this same water. It takes us an hour to reach our pound nets off the western shore. I watch as young Stephen maneuvers around a buoy. A short way off, a fish hawk is screaming from her nest on top of a piling. I watch the boy smile up at the bird and I think: it's happening again. Here's a new generation of water men finding some private, secret satisfaction on the bay.

"I'll take it now, Steve," I say.

Stephen jumps off his basket and runs out to the deck to peer down into the net as we draw alongside. Fishing with a pound net is an old Indian trick. Stretching out from shore for almost five hundred yards is a line of pine poles that we cut and drove into the mud of the bay. Tied to the poles is a long, tapering net that guides fish into smaller and smaller heart-shaped pounds, until they reach the last one, the pocket. Every day except Sunday we come here to haul our catch from the pocket.

I tie up outside the net and join Steve and his father on deck. We can't see what the pocket holds. One thing about fishing, you never know what's going to be in your net. Sometimes there's almost nothing and you don't even meet expenses. But if the blues or alewives are running, that pocket can hold thousands of fish. Steve laughs as a cormorant surfaces from within the net and tries to fly off. That old bird is so stuffed he can barely flop away. "I bet he's been gorging on blues, Poppop!" Steve says to me.

If Steve is right, there'll be a good harvest today. The blue can be three feet long and he usually travels in schools. That fish is lots of mischief. His teeth are rows of razors and he snaps at anything that moves. When he's in a feeding frenzy he will cut and tear and slash, and then force up what's in his belly so he can gorge some more.

Lemuel unties the skiff that we tow behind the *Agnes Elizabeth*, and rows it over the top rim of the net until he is inside the pocket. Lemuel reaches down with a hook, grabs one strand of net and manhandles it up into the skiff. Over and over Lemuel bunts the net, shrinking the diameter until the fish are drawn close to the side of the *Agnes Elizabeth*. Now I can see thousands of fish flashing in the morning sun. I make out a few yellow-fin trout and jellyfish, but mostly—as Steve had guessed—blues.

I start up the hydraulic spool that powers the big bailing net we use to bring our catch aboard. With the spool whining, I swing the bailing net over the deck and plunge the draw string. A river of salt-smelling fish thuds aboard. The boy and I wade up to the top of our boots through leaping, thrashing fish, picking them up with thick gloves and tossing them into the baskets.

When the pocket is empty, Lemuel reties the skiff and climbs aboard. It's time to head home.

As we start back, the thought returns: What is it that pulls Lewis men and boys to the water? Part of the draw certainly is the generations themselves, father and son working together. I was on the water when I was still in grade school, setting a trotline weekends or dredging for oysters on my father's bug-eye when we still worked under sail. The older men taught us to respect the water, knowing the risks but knowing the riches too.

The riches had nothing to do with cash in the bank. We never had much money when I was a boy, but there was always fish to eat, and you could grow things and go duck hunting. I remember the platters my mother put on the table, rounded off with oysters and crab cakes and black duck, served up with corn and beans and tomatoes from her garden.

But the sea is more than the living it provides. It's in the blood. It's a relationship with the Lord. Out here on the water God is somehow closer. You can come to know Him. Really know Him, I mean, not just visit Him once a week. I know this because I've heard Him. Heard Him right out here.

There, off to starboard now, is the spot where our boy drowned. Bud went down just four months after he became a father. But he died doing what he always wanted to do. I can't remember a time when Bud hadn't wanted to be on the bay. He built four boats before he was out of high school, though the one that went down was a commercial fisher from the shipyard. I helped Bud finance that boat. He had her loaded with the latest safety gear: depth finder, auxiliary pump, ship-to-ship radio, all designed to help in the bay's hard blows and sudden fogs.

Bud's boat wasn't lost in a storm or fog. She exploded. We had gasoline engines instead of diesel back in the early sixties, and the way we figured it later, there could have been a leak in the fuel pump, letting fumes build up in the bilge. One spark from a loose plug was all it would take after that. Bud had two crew with him that morning—his brother Lemuel, twelve at the time and skinny as a needlefish, and Bud's friend Arvie. The explosion threw Arvie into the water. Bud and Lem tried to reach the life preservers, but the flames were too hot, so they threw empty gas cans into the water and then jumped overboard. They got a can to Arvie, who was almost unconscious. For a while the three huddled together, praying.

"Lem," said Arvie after a bit, "my time has come."

Bud looked at Arvie, whose leaky can had begun to sink. "Lem," Bud said, "you're lighter than Arvie. How 'bout you swap cans with him?"

So young Lemuel gave the older boy his gasoline can. Our son Bud stayed afloat just a few minutes longer, then went down. In a moment his friend Arvie followed. When help finally came, little Lemuel was near gone too.

When Lemuel, badly burned, was brought ashore by a crabber, my wife, Rosa, raced him to the hospital while I rounded up equipment to drag the bay for the boys' bodies. About thirty fishing boat captains from all over the bay showed up to help find Bud and Arvie. I appreciated that, but I wanted to find my boy myself, without help from anybody. Up until then I thought anything there was to do I could do it. Alone.

We found Arvie early the next day but it looked like we weren't going to find Bud. Again and again the flotilla of fishing boats crisscrossed the bay. I took one of the boats that Bud himself had built and went back and forth, back and forth, always asking God to let me be the one to find my boy.

"Do you have to do it by yourself?"

The voice was as clear as that and I knew I'd just heard the Lord speak.

There is a time, He was saying, when it's right to be self-reliant, and there's a time to give up trying to do everything yourself. Did I have to find Bud with no one helping? "No," I said, very soft. "Just as long as we find him, Lord. I don't have to do it alone anymore."

At that very moment one of the men in another boat hooked onto a piece of Bud's clothing. They brought our boy to the surface and I sailed over to bring him in. I never in my life wanted more to take him in my arms, not even when he was a baby. I laid Bud on the deck and brought him back in the boat he built.

After that day, nothing was ever the same for me. I had learned that the most resourceful man in the world isn't as big as the bay; out on the bay I had learned how small I was.

Up ahead now is Tyler's Cove. I can see our truck coming down the road with Rosa at the wheel; she'll drive with me to the market up in Cambridge. Lem and Steve have finished sorting the catch, and Steve's standing in the bow watching a heron stalk the shore. The bird stabs his beak into the water and comes up with a fish. The old heron will never get rich any more than we will, but the look in his eye says he's doing what he's designed to do.

That's what helped me and Rosa and Bud's widow most—to know that Bud had been doing the thing he most wanted to do.

Isn't that why we Lewises come onto the water generation after generation? It's a living, yes, but it's a lot more than that. There's pain but there's a kind of completion too. Men don't stay on the bay unless they're built for the life. Like that old heron. Like Bud.

Like young Steve. As we pull up to the wharf at Tyler's Cove, Lem jumps onto the dock. Steve tosses him a line. Then the boy turns toward me and comes out with the question I knew he'd be asking me one day.

"Poppop," Steve asks, very serious, "this summer when school's out, would you be needing a boy on board?"

I put my hand on the lad's shoulder and we step off the gently swaying *Agnes Elizabeth* onto the dock where his grandmother is waiting.

"Well, I might, Steve," I say. "If he's a hardworking boy."

Sometimes it takes other people to open our eyes to the wonders around us.

MRS. SHALLOW GOES TO SCHOOL

I remember that as I walked for the first time across the goat pasture to the little African school where I was to teach English, the headmaster's voice sailed across the mud walls.

"This are a pencils!"

"This are a pencils!" fifty young voices shouted back, and I knew I had my work cut out for me.

The Ugandan government, on reaching independence two months before, had decided that English was to be used in all schools in place of the dozens of tribal languages, and it was to help with this that I had volunteered.

I was especially interested in this school, for it had not been built by the government or a foreign mission, but by African Christians in the little community of Salaama. With its thick mud walls and grass roof, it looked like any other house in Salaama, except that in a tree by the door hung a bicycle wheel-rim which was banged with a stone at the start and end of the school day.

Now as I got closer, a little girl ran up to me, snatched my pocketbook, and raced back toward the school with me in hot pursuit. I caught up with her in the doorway, whereupon she dropped to her knees and held up the purse to me on both hands.

I learned later that it is considered beneath the dignity of a teacher to carry anything, and that children habitually kneel when presenting something to an adult. But for the moment I was completely nonplused.

The headmaster, Mr. Muwanga, came to the door and delivered a long speech in Luganda which I took to be the official welcome to my new assignment, but later learned was the daily hello. Then he showed me proudly through the school's three rooms, where a hundred and fifty children, ages six to sixteen, sat on backless board benches. The floor was earth, spread *weekly*, he stressed, with fresh goat dung to keep down the dust. The walls stopped at about four feet, sticks embedded in them supported the roof. This arrangement, of course, let in rain as well as light, but later I noticed that whereas I would jump at the first drop, the children would work on, oblivious to a floor gradually turning to mud beneath their feet.

And yet, I reflected, watching Mr. Muwanga's pride in the physical plant, this was the first headmaster I'd known who had built his school with his own two hands. In each room Mr. Muwanga introduced me. But alas for "Sherrill"! The sounds "r" and "l" are difficult for many Africans and each time the name that came back was "Mrs. Shallow."

I started teaching there three mornings a week and before long I began to fear that the name was only too true. Like the morning when I found the entire school outdoors, busily digging in the ground. A particular species of termite had hatched in the night and the children were hoping to find enough for their mothers to make stew. They could not resist nibbling a little of their catch, however, and every now and then an especially juicy crunch would send a shiver of revulsion through me.

I got a glimpse of the fact that this was shallowness in me a few days later. I had been talking about protein, which is lacking in diets here, but when I came to the word *cheese* could find no equivalent in the local language. It became clear that, in spite of the goats wandering in and out of the classrooms, goat cheese—cheese of any kind—was unknown in this society.

So I told them I would bring some to school with me. I chose a lovely piece of very mild yellow cheddar. But! No sooner had I unwrapped it than every person in the room—children and teachers alike—clapped his hand to his nose. Offended, I put a piece in my mouth to demonstrate how delicious it was. Thereupon I saw in every face the identical reaction of horror I had felt at their insect eating.

Cheese . . . termites . . . two excellent sources of protein, with only custom and familiarity dictating our choice.

Sometimes the children picked up attitudes of mine that I was hardly aware I had. The school opened each day with prayer and Bible reading in Luganda. One day I asked if anyone knew in what language the Bible had originally been written. Every hand went up; that was easy: English!

So I launched into a description of the great age of the Bible, a difficult idea in a country with a written history only a hundred years old. I told them that the Old and New Testaments had been written in different languages and I mentioned that the New Testament represented God seen more clearly, salvation realized, ultimate truth.

Wondering if they understood, I asked the same question a week later. One little girl sprang up confidently: the Old Testament was written in English, the New Testament in American.

The thought haunted me. Was I insisting on American ways and values instead of looking for Christ as He reveals Himself in Africa?

I remembered an episode during my first month at the school. I had assigned the Beatitudes for memory work, using the Basic English Bible, "Happy are they . . . ," and the room was full of silent concentration when suddenly a tall boy in the rear of the room leaped to his feet and cried out something in Luganda. Another boy began to clap, a third beat out a rhythm on the bench. Soon the whole class was on its feet, Mr. Muwanga as well, shuffling and stamping and swaying.

I was enchanted. But I kept thinking: at this rate we will never learn the Beatitudes.

The dance stopped as suddenly as it had begun and the children settled back to work. "What," I asked Mr. Muwanga, "was that?"

"Oh," he said, "that was a dance for the Beatitudes."

I thought of Sunday schools I had sat in, classes intoning "Happy are they" with faces like doom, and decided perhaps these children had learned the Beatitudes better than I knew.

I often brought an ambitious pile of books, maps and diagrams to school—it seemed to me there was so much information to get across in addition to English. And then one day I received a book I hadn't expected. It was a scrapbook made by a sixth grade Sunday school class in Racine, Wisconsin, who had read about this trip in *Guideposts* and sent it "to someone in Africa." On one page they had pasted pictures of children all over the world—a Chinese boy with a kite, a blondhaired child with a ball, and so on.

But when I took the scrapbook down to the school every child there seized on something I had not noticed at all. The African child, wonder of wonders, was not beating a drum or throwing a spear. He was reading a book. The children ran from one to another with the amazing page, marveling and proud. Mr. Muwanga said nothing at all for a long time and when he looked up I thought there were tears in his eyes.

"So that is how they think of us in America," he said softly. "And I never knew." From that day on, it seemed to me, the whole school stood a little straighter.

But it was Mrs. Shallow who learned most from that page of pictures. It was not facts these people needed from Americans. It never is. It was the experience of being liked.

The little girl rushing to carry my handbag on my first day at school, Mr. Muwanga's elaborate welcoming and good-by rituals each day, were part of the African's genius for human relations. And it is this that I will remember when I have forgotten the muddy floors and sagging walls.

I will remember how the children banded together to keep mosquitoes off me, knowing that I was bothered by them.

I will remember the mothers of the children, waiting along the road to school, babies strapped to their backs, voluminous cotton dresses sweeping the ground, holding out to me in both hands an egg or a bunch of bananas. We had no common language between us, but what they could achieve in friendship with a handful of fruit was a school in itself.

And I will remember the party given to honor us. We were all there, Mr. and Mrs. Shallow, Scott, Donn and Elizabeth. They sang tribal songs, they danced, they gave us food, and then Saagala, the school's best pupil, put into two sentences the African gift for relationships.

"We do not call you teacher," he said, "because it sounds too far away. We call you our parents and our brothers and sister, because you have sat down and looked into our hearts."

Elizabeth

*When we don't perceive God in the passing moment, perhaps
it's because we've allowed no room for . . .*

DIVINE INTERRUPTIONS

Often after my lunch I take a brisk walk down a nearby
lane with the intriguing name of Hog Hill Road. It's a
constitutional and I have clocked it with some care so that
it takes just half an hour and I return breathing heavily
and filled with a sense of aerobic accomplishment.

One day several months ago, however, I invited my
eight-year-old son, Donn, to walk with me.

What a difference! First, Donn had some dogs he
wanted to invite. Then there was a culvert he had to
explore. And at last he sidetracked me altogether by
plunging down an old logging road. Long before we
returned, I was aware of an emotion that astonished—
even frightened—me. Instead of being delighted with
these inventive detours I came back frustrated and angry.

Why should this be? Had I become so conditioned to
driving toward a goal that I resisted interruptions automatically, even creative ones?

Now that I was aware of this tendency in myself, I began
observing it everywhere. I watched Tib hanging towels on
the backyard clothesline so purposefully that she would
not glance at some really spectacular gymnastics by a pair

of squirrels. I watched a commuter look up in annoyance when a question interrupted his crossword puzzle. I watched a secretary struggle with impatience when a new girl timidly approached her for help.

To resist interruptions is an instinct we are born with, as anyone knows who has ever had to take a child out of a sandbox. But we Americans have somehow turned this natural reaction into a national virtue. From their earliest days we teach children to concentrate on the task at hand: my eleven-year-old son Scott, for example, wins highest praise from me when he plows through his homework at a single sitting. And I recall the golden rule of my own school days:

"To succeed, choose a goal, then steer dead ahead."

And, of course, there's a great deal to be said for this approach. A person who gives in too easily to interruptions places himself at the mercy of every chance distraction. I once had a secretary for exactly three days, the length of time it took me to discover that she had not completed a single assignment. A telephone call, a special delivery letter, a messenger bringing proofs, any interruption gripped this girl's attention and derailed her train of thought so thoroughly that she never managed to get back to the matter at hand. She would let interruptions interrupt her interruptions until she was hopelessly lost in a tangle of unfinished projects.

Driving toward a goal does prevent this kind of inefficiency. But far too often something unpleasant happens to us along the way. We are no longer driving, we are driven. We become so goal-centered that we lose our sense of the values that dictated the goal in the first place.

Following my detour-filled walk with Donn I began to wonder if there was an art to handling interruptions creatively.

I decided to reread the Gospels from a special viewpoint: how had Jesus handled this problem? Right away I made a fascinating discovery: how much of His work was accomplished during "interruptions"!

Once Jesus was on His way to the house of a highly placed Jewish leader, Jairus, whose twelve-year-old daughter was desperately ill. Speed was essential—and just at that point an ailing woman touched the hem of His garment. How did Jesus respond to the interruption? He stopped. He searched the throng until He found the woman. He took time to make certain that she grasped the significance of what had happened to her. Sure enough, He reached the twelve-year-old's bedside "too late" in the view of her frantic family. But in fact He was right on time, His own perfect time, to restore her to her awestruck parents.

Jesus was making His final entrance into Jerusalem. Awaiting Him was the most important hour in human history. And then . . . a blind beggar stopped Him. People tried to silence the beggar, but Jesus heard him. He interrupted His all-important journey, talked to the man, healed him.

So the first thing that I observed was that Jesus held interruptions in respect. When one came, He gave it His full attention. It was as if He did not think of these episodes as random distractions, but as part of the divine pattern.

Next, however, I noticed that Jesus always returned to His original goal. Nowhere did I find that an interruption kept Him from doing what He had set out to accomplish.

Jesus had an almost equal respect for goals and for interruptions. What made this possible?

It was, I think, that Jesus saw His life from the perspective of eternity.

I remember my sense of excitement when I first realized this. Jesus literally had all the time there was, so it didn't matter if a trip or a sermon or a meal was interrupted. After His earthly death He would continue His loving involvement with mankind. Whether He pressed toward a particular goal or whether He paused and listened for the hidden message of an interruption, He did so from the viewpoint of forever.

And so should I.

If, as a Christian, I believe in an eternal life of joyful service, then I must reflect this view in my present life. I must be alert to the opportunity inherent in an interruption. My little Elizabeth doesn't come knocking on my door in the middle of my work-time by accident: if I squelch her I will miss what she has to communicate. And my boy Donn has much to tell me when he looks into a culvert or urges me to strike off into the woods.

In fact, a few weeks after I took Donn on that first walk we set out again in the evening. This time, it was I who suggested that we make a detour. We were walking down Hog Hill Road at a good rate when suddenly, with a great flurry of feathers, a bird flapped ponderously out of the evening sky and disappeared into the hollow of an old apple tree.

I hesitated . . . but it was just for a moment.

"Come on, Donn," I said. "Let's have a look at an owl's house."

You should have seen the light in his eyes. It was, I believe, reflected from eternity.

John

It's a humble kind of food, but this
French farmer praises God for . . .

SAUERKRAUT!

Paul Frank tells his story to John

Sauerkraut! Wonderful sauerkraut.

It was time for the noon break. The rest of the workers had already left and I couldn't wait to get home too: today Lise was serving *choucroute,* the national dish of Alsace: meat and potatoes heaped on top of the world's best sauerkraut. We know; making sauerkraut is our business.

I walked through puddles on the hosed-down concrete floor of our processing shed here in Entzheim in northeastern France, inhaling the tart sauerkraut tang. On either side of me a bubbly mousse rose to the top of huge fermentation pits. Over my head threads of fresh cabbage hung from the conveyer belt. Against the wall, bags of sea salt. A layer of shredded cabbage, a layer of salt. That's all there is to sauerkraut.

Five minutes later I pulled up in front of our house, next door to the sprawling half-timbered building where my father and mother live and where Grandfather and Great-grandfather lived before them. During my childhood that building was part barn, part quarters-for-farm-workers, part missionary rest-stop, but most of all, our home, where four generations of Franks lived in rooms around the courtyard. My three sisters and I grew up there surrounded by chickens and goats and the *sshwwtt-sshwwtt* of cows' milk going into a pail. I'm just old enough now, at forty-four, to understand the consternation I caused when I broke tradition by moving away. Four feet away, right next door, but away.

"I'm home!" I called as I walked through the front door of the much smaller house I'd built for Lise and me. Our three daughters, teenagers Miriam and Estelle and seven-year-old Dorcas, were already home from school for the noontime main meal of the day. All three ran to hug me, then vanished back into the kitchen from which wafted the mouth-watering smell of *choucroute*. Lise appeared in the doorway, longfork in her hand.

"Almost ready, Paul!"

I stepped into the closet-sized front room Lise and I use for our business office. The computer was up, its green cursor blinking at me: seventeen-year-old David, our only son, must be home too. David's a natural at electronics; he doesn't know yet whether he will come back here to the farm when he's finished at the university.

If he doesn't, it will be another break with tradition, the biggest in a family pattern dating back a hundred years. But David's generation faces choices none before his ever did. Just outside our front door is a *sabot*, an outsized wooden shoe. It sits there on our small lawn today as a decoration, but when I was a boy that was a working shoe and there wasn't any question who was to do the working.

I was. And my sisters. And everyone else in the village. By the time I was seven, I was already walking the cabbage to make sauerkraut.

Right across the street is where I did it, in that brick building. Looking out the window I could almost feel those cold autumn afternoons. After school when we were laying down a *couche* of sauerkraut, I'd come home, gulp a mug of hot milk, then join the other boys and girls and the old men and women in that brick "factory."

I could still see my father drive his steel-wheeled tractor up to the door, pulling a flatbed wagon piled high with yellow-green cabbages cut just a few minutes earlier from the fields behind our home. The older women from the neighborhood cored the cabbage with sharp semi-circular knives, then shredded the heads while men who could no longer work in the fields forked the shreds evenly into a vat big enough to swallow Dad's tractor, wagon and all. Another man spread salt over the top of each layer.

That's when we children's work began. We put on the heavy wooden shoes and climbed down a ladder into the *cuve* to walk up and down the salted cabbage driving out the air. Back and forth. Back again. Wait while the men turn the uppermost layer with a pitchfork and re-salt. Resume walking.

It was hard work but there was no thought of doing otherwise. As we trudged to and fro the history of the Rhine basin swirled around us in the mix of languages we spoke. This Rhine bottomland has switched back and forth again and again between Germany and France. My grandfather spoke French as his first language. Then Alsace became German and my father's first language was German. French, German, it didn't matter because everyone also spoke Alsatian. We considered ourselves half French, half German and three-quarters Alsatian.

I could hear Lise and the three girls putting dishes on the table out in the kitchen. Lise, the girl who hurled the snowball at me . . .

I was twenty-one years old at the time, still unmarried, and all around me the family marriage machinery was cranking into gear. Finding a suitable wife had always been a family affair. When my father started coming up with names, however, I objected.

"Dad," I said, "people find their own wives today." Dad stared at me. "When I was fourteen," I went on, "I started asking God to show me the right girl, and I know He will."

When Dad heard that I'd been praying for seven years, he nodded and dropped the subject. He could live with change as long as important things stayed the same, and prayer was at the top of his list of what was important. My parents prayed for everything. For me and my sisters, for the farmhands, for the wholesalers at the market. They prayed for the animals, and for rain—but not too much rain, please.

That's the way I was raised. By the time I was old enough to work in the fields with the adults, I knew that I would be running this farm some day. And by age fourteen it seemed natural to start praying for the right wife to do it with me. It wouldn't be easy, being married to an Alsatian farmer. My wife would feed the animals, cook for family and hired hands, sew, put up vegetables, work next to me in the fields. So it was a tall order and of course I asked God's help.

One wintry day when I was twenty-one I drove up to our church's retreat in the Vosges mountains. As I came around the bend, a well-thrown snowball splattered all over my windshield. Beside the road I saw a young girl laughing. Even with her woolen cap hiding part of her face, I could see that she was gorgeous.

"That's the girl I am going to marry."

I knew it just as surely as though the words were written in the melting snow on my windshield.

Lise, my snowball thrower, turned out to be the sixteen-year-old daughter of a cabbage farmer from a village a few kilometers from ours. Every spare moment of that young people's weekend, I sought her out. We crowded a year's worth of talk into forty-eight hours. Two days after the snowball incident I asked Lise if she would ever consider marrying a farmer and she said yes. Then I asked her if she would ever consider marrying *me* and she said yes.

It took longer to get a yes from Lise's family. Her father was adamant that we not see one another for an entire year. At the end of that time Lise would be seventeen, a grown woman. If she still wished it, he wouldn't object to my starting to court her.

So a year later I began making regular trips to Lise's village. That was twenty-two years ago and Lise and I have walked every step of the way together ever since. Together we took the unheard-of step of building our own house "away" from the family. Together we made the decision to buy more land, nearly doubling the size of our farm. And to take on the financial risk of modernizing our processing operation. Fewer and fewer villagers were showing up to tramp sauerkraut. And so we built a new plant, turned to conveyer belts and clamshell lifts and mechanical shredders and pressers.

In the essential things, however, we haven't broken with tradition. I stepped into the parlor where I could look out the back window over our flat brown land. The soil here is seven meters deep! Out there each spring Lise and I and the children, all six of us, climb onto the gang planter and, with a hired hand driving, set off across the fields toward the line of poplar trees in the distance. Lise and I and the two older children face forward, taking tiny green-white cabbage shoots out of a tray and placing them into the slowly rotating planter wheels. When we miss a slot the two little girls are there, sitting backwards, facing us with their own transplant trays, waiting to fill the gap. It's a time for singing as we chug toward the wheeling crows rising from the poplars. But all the while Lise and I keep up a series of silent prayers. We pray for each tender shoot as it goes into the soil. Forty thousand cabbages, forty thousand prayers.

Together Lise and I have walked through the hard times of farm life. It was Lise who sat round the clock at nine-year-old David's bedside after that awful morning when he fell into the conveyer belt. I'd been working here in the office when the phone rang.

"Paul, come quick." It was one of our workers, panic in

his voice. "David's hurt. We've called the ambulance. It's bad."

David was lying on a table with a blanket around him when I got to the processing shed.

"Hi, Dad!" He tried to smile, his face as white as a cabbage seedling. Lifting the blanket, I saw that his left arm was hanging onto his shoulder by a thread. He had slipped on the damp concrete and fallen into the moving chain assembly. It's a wonder David survived at all, but with the marvel of microscopic surgery, with hundreds of hours of physical therapy and just plain toughing it out, David today can keep up with his friends in a pushup contest.

"Dinner!" Lise sang out. I didn't need calling twice. How much a part of our lives was this kitchen table where we gathered each noon, the six of us. "Bon appétit!" said Lise, setting down a platter she could hardly lift. On it was an astonishing mound of steaming sauerkraut smothered with sausage and smoked pork loins and ham and bacon. Side plates of bread and potatoes boiled in the skin. Sharp mustard, homemade gherkins. *Choucroute!*

We sat down and Lise heaped our plates high. No one objected. Sauerkraut is healthy fare, so rich a source of vitamin C that Christopher Columbus carried it with him in 1492 to ward off scurvy in his crew.

Our plates are served. It's time for the blessing. Every head at the table is bowed, except my own. As I pray I look out our back window to the fields where we grow a hundred and fifty acres of cabbage.

"Thank You, Father, for the hands that prepared this."

For answering the prayers of a fourteen-year-old boy for the perfect wife.

"Thank You for each of our children." *For songs to sing as the seedlings go into the ground.*

"Thank You for helping David make the right decision about his future." *For the important things that stay the same in the midst of change.* The children are getting impatient! "In Jesus' name, Amen."

Six pairs of hands dive in, and we begin. To myself, however, I add one more prayer, a very personal one. *Thank You, God, for sauerkraut.*

*In the ordinary events of every day she came to
see the extraordinary love of God . . .*

A GIFT NAMED MOLLY

It was late when I drove up to the motel, but the question uppermost in my mind was not whether there was a vacancy. Rather I wondered who would greet me at the desk. What special person would it be? What encounter, however brief, was about to enrich my life?

Before that evening, such thoughts would never have entered my mind. But then, before that evening I hadn't received my gift . . .

Earlier that day, I'd driven the two hundred miles to Millersville, Pennsylvania, wondering all the way why I'd said yes to this assignment. The woman I was to interview was forty-three years old, mother of six, and she was dying of cancer.

Doubtless she was brave and humorous and faith-filled and all the things the *Guideposts* reader who had suggested the story said she was. But I was sure I would drive away from meeting Molly Shelley feeling guilty. Untimely death always seemed to me to imply a burden, to require of the rest of us that we become somehow more worthy of the gift of life.

From Millersville I followed the directions Molly had

given me over the phone, past stone barns and cornfields to an area of ranch-style homes: "Ours is the one where the grass needs mowing."

I wove my way past bikes and baseball bats in the driveway and parked at the back of the house. I was starting around to the front when a slender woman—too slender I saw at once—appeared in the kitchen door and said, "Come this way! Then you won't be company."

In the kitchen a tow-headed little boy was building a fort with wooden blocks. But—although Molly had suggested I stay for supper—nothing else appeared to be going on in the kitchen.

She led me into the living room, moving briskly, and I commented on how well she seemed. "Oh, I feel so much better since they stopped the chemotherapy. It wasn't helping and it lowers resistance. I had to wear shoes even indoors! Don't you love the feel of a rug beneath your toes?"

I looked down at the shag carpet and confessed with shame that I'd never noticed.

"Oh, but you must! You must notice everything! Would you believe," she went on, "that I never saw trees until last summer? Never really looked at them—how the branches grow, how many shades of green there are."

I had not been prepared for her enthusiasm. All the external signs of illness were there: the loose-hanging cotton dress, the thinning hair. But this woman was vibrantly alive. "This noticing," I said, "did it begin after you . . ."

"After I found out I was dying?" Molly supplied for me. "That's right. Before that, I was too worried about what people thought of *me* to notice much of anything else. I was running around trying to be the perfect wife, the perfect Christian, the perfect housekeeper."

I glanced at the roller skates in the middle of the room. "Molly, I've been admiring you just because you seem so *un*worried about the impression you're making. This visit of mine, for example. You didn't put on make-up or rush around getting magazine edges straight, just because a guest was coming."

The change in Molly's outlook had begun a year and a half ago, she said, when a man she scarcely knew came to visit her in the hospital. She'd gone there for a "ruptured appendix." Emergency surgery had revealed instead advanced and inoperable cancer. Molly lay in a high-sided hospital bed adjusting to the news . . . and to the novel experience of doing nothing. With a husband in a demanding job as a research physicist and six children, then ages four to sixteen, her days had been a scramble of activities.

"I believed that my life came to me as a gift from God—and therefore I had to accomplish as much with it as I could."

I nodded, remembering my identical thought on the drive down here. It was true, wasn't it? God must demand some accounting, after all, for the lives He's given us!

Molly had lain fretfully in that hospital bed, thinking about the Bible study she always attended that night, and the elderly lady she visited afterward, when she was startled by the sound of weeping from the foot of her bed. A gray-haired man stood there, tears rolling down his lined face unchecked. A stream of friends had passed through the room since the start of visiting hours, but this was someone Molly scarcely knew. A janitor at one of the local schools, she seemed to recall. He appeared occasionally at a prayer meeting Molly and her husband attended. Randizi! That was his name!

What terrible thing could have happened to him, Molly wondered, that he was sobbing this way? There were tubes down her throat, so in silence she asked God, Why is Mr. Randizi crying?

Because he loves you.

The answer was so unexpected that she actually laughed. ("A bad idea with stitches in your stomach.") There was no reason why Mr. Randizi should love her: I've never done a single thing for him!

You didn't have to. He loves you because you are lovable.

After a while Mr. Randizi wiped his eyes and relinquished the spot at the bedside to the next visitor. But the wonder of that silent revelation remained with Molly. It accompanied her home from the hospital, stayed with her as she helped her husband, Don, and their children come to terms with her early death. Me? Molly? Lovable just as I am—even if it's not perfect?

The silent dialogue with God, begun in the hospital, continued.

Come out in the yard with Me, she heard Him say one day.

Now? But I haven't cleared the breakfast table or—

Now.

Outside, summer green showed on every bough. Green? Why, green was not one color! Three, four . . . she counted ten separate shades that until that moment she had labeled "green." God had made each one different. Each glorious.

The telephone called her back inside. A talkative neighbor. There was an extra long cord on Molly's kitchen phone; she had the breakfast things in the dishwasher before she heard Him.

A few minutes ago you saw My individual colors. On the other end of this phone is something more special still, a human being unique in all the world.

So it had gone all that day. Stop! Look! Savor the wonder of each moment. When sixteen-year-old Christopher banged through the back door, broad-shouldered and serious, Molly thought: I missed his childhood because I was straightening the linen shelves.

When Corinne shouted over the roar of the vacuum cleaner, "Mother, will you hear my spelling words later?" Molly bent down and switched off the machine.

"I'll hear them now," she said.

How long, Molly wondered, had God Himself been trying to get her attention over the roar of activities? Why had it taken a fatal illness to make her listen?

But now that she was listening, the message was dazzlingly clear. The green of the leaves, the neighbor's phone call, the moments with Don and her children, each of these things was a unique and undeserved gift from God Himself. He gave them not because she was good, not because she had earned them, but because He loved her.

It was a message that would change a lifelong pattern

of being busy because she wasn't satisfied being herself. Of overdoing, of trying to deserve God's approval by living up to some never-never standard of perfection. If Greg's tuba was on the floor when the doorbell rang, she let it lie there. God loved her!

He loved her so much He'd given her a world of wonders. Colors and trees and rugs beneath her toes. And most of all, the people in her world.

"I had it backward, you see. I thought my life was a gift. Now I know He never gave my life to me at all."

Your life is not My gift to you, God told her. *It is My gift to Don. And to Mr. Randizi, and to the old lady you visit, and to the grocery clerk . . .*

(And to me, Molly! I thought as I listened to her. You don't know what a shining, beautiful, glorious gift you are to me, just sitting there with delight in your eyes and dust on your furniture . . .)

"It's other people's lives," Molly went on, "that are God's gifts to me. Not one limited, narrow little life, but hundreds and hundreds of lives, and the whole world around me—that's how much He loves me! That's the size of His gift!"

Glimpsing that love, Molly said, learning to recognize His gifts as they arrived moment by moment, was making the approach of death less fearful: "Death must be a gift too—the biggest of all. I mean, if He's so lavish on this earth, what must heaven be!"

Meanwhile, by accepting God's love, Molly had become the self-confident and joyful and undefensive person God was giving to me at this moment. "You see," she said, "if I'm His gift to someone else, then I must be okay! God wouldn't give discards or rejects. He gives good gifts!"

As the older children drifted home from ball fields and summer jobs, we began a sociable preparation of supper. As Franz put on the water for spaghetti, he told me about the farmer he worked for. Judith and I put the ice in the glasses while she told me about her plans to become a writer.

They knew they were losing their mother. Even five-year-old Tim knew. And yet they were as bubbling and outgoing as any children I know.

Dr. Donald Shelley came home from work and made the salad. Then the nine of us gathered around the table. We talked about church and baseball and death and model airplanes.

The comment that summed it all up, though, was Molly's. "Just think!" she said to me over ice cream and blueberry syrup. "God loved me so much He gave me you!"

I was surprised, because I hadn't done anything at all (unless you count the ice in the glasses). And then I remembered. I didn't have to do anything.

It was late, as I say, when I finally got back in my car. But I looked forward to meeting whoever would be behind that motel desk. As for the long drive home the following day—well, I had a lot of trees to look at along the way.

Elizabeth

Postscript: Several months after this story appeared in Guide-posts, *I went to see Molly again. By then she was no longer able to get out of bed, so we visited in her bedroom. On the wall hung a red felt banner with a design of balloons stitched onto it.*

"My shroud," Molly explained. "I made it myself."

Everyone coming to the funeral, she said, would be given a balloon. "Then at the graveside they'll let them go. They'll rise up, up—oh I wish I didn't have to miss it!"

I was out of the country when Molly died several months later. But one of her friends wrote to describe the scene: hundreds of balloons soaring into a cloudless sky. I don't believe Molly missed a minute of it.

E.

TV commentator, world-roving journalist,
he documented the abundant society his father dreamed of.
Then he and his wife discovered . . .

THE JOY OF DOING WITH LESS

Outside the tiny village of Robertsbridge, England, John stopped the car while we inspected one another. John's tie was straight, my white gloves spotless, our clothes as wrinkle-free as drip-dry things ever get. Still . . . I pulled out a comb and gave my hair an anxious swipe.

We'd been invited to lunch at the home of Britain's most celebrated journalist, Malcolm Muggeridge—doubtless some daunting mansion with a mile-long driveway and a butler at the door.

We drove all the way through Robertsbridge, however—a matter of two minutes—without seeing such a house. John turned around and, getting directions from a postman on a bicycle, we stopped in front of a small brick cottage. A ruddy-faced white-haired man straightened up from the garden he'd been weeding.

"Just in time!" he cried. "Kitty's heating up the soup!"

In the kitchen a handsome woman with graying hair tied in a bun at her neck was setting bowls on a bare wooden table.

"Could you slice the bread?" she said. As I did (gloves stuffed in my pocket), she took a platter of cheese from the refrigerator.

This was their lunch menu every day of the week, she told me: vegetable soup, whole wheat bread, cheese, yogurt. It was so good John and I could understand why they'd never want to change it!

The other two meals, they told us, were equally standard. For breakfast, prunes, All-Bran, bread spread with honey from the hives they showed us at the rear of the garden. For supper, scrambled eggs—from their own hens of course—vegetables from the garden, Kitty's homemade oatcakes.

"When I think of the time I used to spend fretting over what to serve for dinner!" she said. "Chasing down recipes, running out to the market, worrying when we had company about how a dish would turn out . . ."

"Was it to save time," we asked, knowing what a full speaking and writing schedule they maintained, "that you simplified your eating habits?"

Time, yes. "Also to save money." When we looked surprised at this, the Muggeridges enumerated some of the needs they were trying to respond to: a couple who could live luxuriously are living simply "so that others can live at all."

But chiefly, they said, it was to recover a sense of joy in the simple, daily acts of living.

It wasn't just elaborate meals they'd eliminated. The Muggeridges had analyzed their entire life-style and begun a conscious effort to pare down. And the life pattern which resulted, emptier of things, has been fuller by far, they told us, in every other way.

"It's the very opposite," Malcolm Muggeridge said, "of what I was brought up to believe."

Muggeridge's father was a pioneer socialist, an optimist as most people were at the beginning of this century, sure that an age of universal prosperity and bliss was just around the corner. Prosperity and bliss went together: if people just had enough of the material blessings of life, happiness and morality would inevitably follow.

"I remember applauding ecstatically as Dad would mount a soap box on some street corner to expose poverty as the source of mankind's ills. For years I gave up games after school to pass out leaflets heralding a better world."

And of course it came, this better world, to much of Europe and North America. But with it did not come the expected peace and contentment. After the two most savage wars in history, skyrocketing rates of suicide, crime, drug addiction and divorce in the very countries enjoying the greatest prosperity, Malcolm's generation found themselves wondering where materialism had failed.

"I was raised, of course, according to good socialist principles, as an atheist." But his parents kept the New Testament on the coffee table because—even though Jesus could hardly be the Son of a nonexistent God—He was obviously a working man and a socialist. From Malcolm's earliest days Jesus' words held a strange fascination for him. Here seemed to be held out the very opposite of the earthly utopia his father was struggling for.

What shall it profit a man if he gain the whole world and lose his own soul?

Lay not up for yourselves treasures on earth.

In the world ye shall have tribulation (—surely not once the Socialists were in power?—) but be of good cheer: I have overcome the world.

Over and over, intimations of another reality, more enduring than the material.

Strangely enough, the Muggeridges said, the first person they knew who consistently lived this reality was their own son Leonard. Leonard was different almost from babyhood. As a child, when someone asked him what he wanted to be, he would never answer "a fireman" or "an airplane pilot." He always said, "I want to be a Christian." Malcolm and Kitty would look at each other in amazement: where had he even heard the word?

When it came time for his military service, Leonard was in a dilemma because he didn't believe in force as an answer to anything. At last, because it was the law, he entered the Army, but refused to take any rank above private. He volunteered for all the unpleasant duties and as a result spent much of his Army career in the cookhouse. Naturally the other soldiers took advantage of him, even helping themselves to his possessions. Leonard knew perfectly well who had taken his watch and his pen, but he never demanded them back. And curiously, little by little, it was Leonard to whom the entire barracks began to look for leadership—and the watch and pen mysteriously found their way back into his duffle.

Today, his parents said, Leonard and his wife and children are the happiest people they know. "Leonard is a teacher, but he doesn't even understand the current row over pay rises. It's never occurred to him to want more than he has."

Then it was Leonard, we asked, who'd convinced them to experiment with simpler living for themselves?

"Not directly." The immediate impetus had come from a group of men in Nunraw, Scotland. In 1967 the BBC had asked Malcolm Muggeridge to do a documentary on the Cistercian monastery at Nunraw. For three weeks he lived, ate and worshipped with the monks there, and by the end of that time he knew he'd been in touch with a paradox.

"For years the powerful persuaders of our consumer society have been telling us that satiety is the road to happiness. Buy this! Own one of these! Satisfy every appetite!" But on a lonely Scottish hillside, another voice was being listened to. One that said, Deny yourself. Die to the flesh. He who loses his life shall find it.

"These men had given up everything that gives life meaning for most of us: possessions, money, marriage, success, personal pleasure—even privacy." All, including the abbot, lived in a common dormitory. When Muggeridge was waked at 4:00 each morning for 4:30 mass, the monks had already been at prayer for an hour. The meals were Spartan, the work in the fields humble and repetitive.

According to the psychology of gratification, these deprived souls should have been climbing the bare wooden walls. "Yet never in my life had I been among men more truly free, more constantly joyous." The contrast between the joyful monks and the frenzied "normal" world was all too clear. Muggeridge began to wonder if outside a monastery, too, it was possible to divest life of some of the soul-destroying clutter.

He and Kitty began a deliberate program of cutting down. They sold their large automobile for a tiny one that gets forty miles a gallon and seldom needs repairs. They moved from a big house—the stately home we'd looked for in vain—to this cottage that Kitty manages in a quarter of the time she used to devote to housekeeping.

What were some other nonessentials? Tobacco and alcohol were easy economies. Hairdos, Kitty decided, reflecting on the time and money spent at the beauty parlor, were another. She let her hair grow and caught it back in a becoming bun. Both Muggeridges went over their wardrobes and concluded that, if they ignored the caprices of changing styles, they could keep neat, clean and warm for many years with the clothes they already had.

The energy that used to go to planning wardrobes and menus, the time expended shopping for them, the whole relentless hourly slavery to *things*—much of this the Muggeridges have eliminated. They have more time now in their busy lives for reading, for prayer, for each other. For savoring the passing minutes instead of scrambling through them. For enjoying the rattle of rain on the roof, the glint of sunlight on a crockery bowl—the common-place things that get lost in a life of uncontrolled accumulation.

"We're still looking for things we can do without," Kitty said. "Most of all," her husband added, "we hope that our doing with less can mean that some truly deprived person will have more."

Just before our visit to Robertsbridge, Malcolm Muggeridge had been in France filming a television program about a Christian community called L'Arche. Here the mentally disabled, the mongoloid, the insane live together with mentally normal people. During Muggeridge's stay, the World Hunger Conference in Rome was calling attention to the tragic irony of our century: a time when more people are in possession of more goods than ever before is also the century that has seen more people starve than any previous period in history. So Muggeridge asked the residents of L'Arche, "What's the answer?"

As with a single voice these men and women medically classified as incompetents, shouted out:

"*Moins!*" "Less!"

"I'll eat less food!" cried one man. "Turn down the thermostat!" suggested another. "Turn off the lights an hour early!" offered a third.

"I thought to myself," Muggeridge recalled, "who are the insane? The people in here, or the leaders of industry and labor with their constant calls for more?" The supposedly feebleminded had leapt to the heart of the matter, each discovering in his already frugal life a place where he could strip away still more.

The Muggeridges walked us out to our car with a parting gift of fresh-picked raspberries. A couple with all the time in the world for visitors . . . for picking berries . . . for living.

Less! we thought as we waved good-by. The answer for a hungry world. And for those of us whose lives are too full of things, too empty of meaning, the invitation to a personal answer, as well.

Elizabeth

Can we learn to see more of God in the common things of life?
We can if we cultivate . . .

SECRETS OF SIMPLICITY

"Beauty of style and harmony and grace and good rhythm depend upon simplicity." Plato wrote this advice to artists four hundred years before Christ.

Harmony, grace and rhythm in daily living, too, stem from simplicity; strain, tension and disorder from the lack of it.

And yet of all the virtues, modern life seems most lacking in this one. Simplicity seems to belong to an earlier century; as society grows ever more complex, we are "torn in a thousand directions."

Is simplicity possible in today's world, or has it vanished with the sheep from the village green? In the experience of the wisest people we know, simplicity is not only possible but essential to a meaningful life.

The key lies in the word itself. "Simplicity" comes from two Latin words: *sine,* meaning "without," and *plica,* a "fold" in a piece of cloth (as in our word "pleat"). Applied to life-style it signifies life without sharp angles or changes in direction, life-in-a-straight-line—no matter how far that line stretches. For simplicity does not demand that life be rustic or urban, rich or poor, married or single, only that it go in a single direction. Its opposite is multiplicity, "many-folded" or many-angled living.

Although St. Paul lived in what we imagine to have been less hectic times, it is hard to imagine a life more full of variety than his. Constantly on the move amid new scenes and faces, constantly drawn into local squabbles and divisions, thwarted in his intentions by weather and shipping schedules, plagued by personal health problems, he was expected to be preacher, teacher, healer and correspondent to hundreds.

And yet he was able to write to his friends at Philippi: "This *one thing* I do . . . I press toward the mark for the prize of the high calling of God in Christ Jesus" (Philippians 3:13-14, KJV, emphasis mine). Because he had a mark, a goal toward which his whole life was directed, all the multitudinous details of the journey made for him a single piece.

Now it's obvious that after leading a helter-skelter existence for years, we can't apply a few rules and overnight find that all the pieces fit. But we can make a start.

CHOOSING THE GOAL

Any goal will simplify life; not every goal will ennoble it. A miser has found simplicity—no thought beyond money complicates his days—but not a simplicity we covet. A person who makes music or baseball or beauty or sex the all-important thing will simplify his life accordingly. The friends he makes, the books he reads, the way he spends his money, even the food he eats will be subordinated to his single goal, and his life will be impoverished or enriched thereby. The two questions each of us must ask as he defines his life goal are:

- What single thing is more important to me than any other?
- Will I stretch to my full height in reaching for it?

STARTING THE DAY WITH PRAYER

Through the centuries, spiritually attuned people have discovered that some form of the purpose "to know God" is the goal which most fully employs every capacity. A morning prayer for simplicity in the day ahead might be:

"Lord, You are the true goal of my life. In the varied business of this day let me never lose sight of You. Show me how to make each of my activities a stepping stone to a closer relationship with You. If any chore or pastime or habit of mine leads in another direction, show me what it is and help me to remove it."

Then look with God at some of your immediate goals (a college education? marriage? writing a book?) to see whether this day's activities form a straight line in that direction. A businesswoman's day doesn't have to consist of a sales meeting *and* a half hour at the track *and* a session with an architect. She jogs *so that* she can do her best on the job *which makes possible* the home she and her husband are building. By seeing how things fit together, what looms like a hodgepodge of unrelated events becomes a unity.

LEARNING TO SAY NO

The reason that simplicity is so hard to achieve in the modern world is not that Western science has given us technology, but that it has given us choice. With machines to handle the commonest, most burdensome chores, real simplification of life is possible for the first time ever.

But by the same token there have never been so many possibilities open to us. A century ago life pretty well limited the choices. For leisure time there was the Wednesday night prayer meeting, the circus once a year and skating as long as the ice lasted. Today we can add skiing, jet travel, watching TV, calling a friend on the phone, zither lessons, photography and hundreds of other options. Life has stopped saying no to us. If we value simplicity we must learn to say no to ourselves.

ADDING BY SUBTRACTING

John and I have found we enjoy evenings out twice as much when we cut our agenda in half. Instead of dinner and the theater we now choose a special restaurant and devote the entire evening to enjoying the meal. On the nights when we have opera tickets we have a stand-up sandwich and with some of the money saved buy the libretto.

PACKAGING OUR TIME

So much of the feeling of multiplicity in our lives comes from an attempt to juggle several activities simultaneously. Years ago my first employer, Robert R. Updegraff, taught me the secret of "packaging" time. "A major mistake we make," he observed, "is to live life as a continuous stream of hours and days rather than as a series of separate Projects and Episodes."

A "project" Updegraff defined as *something definite to be accomplished,* such as getting a meal or writing a letter, while an "episode" is *something to be enjoyed,* a bridge game, a walk in the woods, reading a magazine article. But in either case the key word is "package," drawing a ring around each experience to isolate it from the others.

This month try saying with St. Paul, not only about your life as a whole but about each hour in it: "This one thing I do, *forgetting those things which are behind"* (Philippians 3:13, KJV, emphasis mine).

PARING DOWN THE PROPS

Sooner or later most people who aim at simplicity find themselves whittling away at the sheer mass of things that they've accumulated. The hermit in his cave, the nun in her cell, have rid themselves of all possessions—not because they were evil, but because they required too much attention.

A woman minister, pastor of seven separate churches in rural Maine and a dear friend of ours, decided that one thing she could simplify was her wardrobe. The endless "what-to-wear" question, the different shoes and handbags for each costume, changing lengths and styles, all of this consumed energy. So Margaret Hendrickson found a dress in a color that she liked and bought six of them: for her the tyranny of clothing was ended.

"Our life is frittered away by detail," wrote Thoreau. "Simplify! Simplify!" In living out his own injunction, Thoreau systematically pared away at externals. "I went to the woods," he writes in *Walden*, "because I wished to live deliberately, to front only the essential facts of life . . . and not, when I came to die, discover that I had not lived."

Not all of us can escape to the woods, but we can be ruthless with belongings that do not aid in the real business of living. A good place to start is with a cluttered desk (or garage, bureau drawer, kitchen shelf). A determined weeding-out of anything you have not actually used in the last year can be the beginning of a new relationship between you and the clamoring world of things.

As you make these experiments in simplicity, end your day as you begin it: by drawing aside with God. Now is the time to bring to Him the day just ended, asking Him to smooth out any wrinkles of irrelevancy that may have crept into the fabric of your life, and to give you for the night ahead the blessing of a single eye.

Elizabeth

PART THREE

SEEING GOD AS OUR GUIDE

To see Him as our Guide is to see Him up close . . . intimately concerned with the events of our lives, leading us in the way love has prepared.

Following Him day by day, hour by hour, we discover why the psalmist could say with perfect trust: The Lord is my Shepherd.

THE WRITERS WHO COULDN'T FIND WORK
What looked like bad news was God's way of getting our attention.

THE YEAR WE STARTED ASKING
We were in lion country, far from civilization, and our car was stuck.

FINDING GUIDANCE IN THE BIBLE
We had a decision to make. Could we find our answer in the Bible?

TOO STRANGE TO BE COINCIDENCE
He was an ordinary kind of man . . . led by an extraordinary God.

WITHOUT KNOWING WHY
Shirley's story: Was loneliness playing tricks with her mind? Terry's story: Five days had passed since the prayer.

LEARNING TO RECEIVE GOD'S GUIDANCE
Seeing more of God as our Guide.

*Religious writing was the last thing we
would have chosen . . .*

THE WRITERS WHO
COULDN'T FIND WORK

The Paris doctor warned us that the baby would never reach full term. And without an abortion, he warned, my own life would be in danger.

Our ears took in the words; our minds refused them. Destroy the child we'd waited for? Thus, after three years of roaming Europe as travel writers, John and I hurried home to the specialist my anxious family had located in New York City.

Only to confront a second crisis. Two major New York newspapers had recently folded; scores of expert writers were out of work. The jobs we applied for had waiting periods before we could even get on a list.

Doctor's bills were mounting and the one resource we had, our writing experience, was worth nothing. The one resource, that is, that we knew about . . . We had no idea, back then in 1950, about the all-sufficiency of God.

Our anxiety had reached the desperation point when John found a stop-gap job. Just until something better turned up, he was to be a reporter for a little sixteen-page religious pamphlet published out of a couple of hotel rooms. He thought the name was *Guideposts*.

"Religious?" I asked incredulously. "Did you tell them we don't go to church or anything?"

He had, but the editor, a man named Len LeSourd, had simply smiled. "God has a plan for you, John, no matter how hard you try to run from it."

The baby was born, full-term and healthy—our son John Scott, now thirty-nine, a country-music writer, a husband and father himself.

And John and I were launched on a lifetime of Christian writing—and the biggest travel adventure of all: the journey of faith. "God has a plan for you . . ." It's true of every human being. Sometimes, when you're as deaf as John and I were, it takes seeming disaster to point it out.

Elizabeth

When we fail to receive God's guidance,
it's often because we fail to ask.

THE YEAR WE
STARTED ASKING

The car gave a violent lurch and came to a stop. "What was that!" the children cried. Tib looked down into the deep draw below us. "I think we've gone through the bridge," she said.

It was true. As soon as I stepped out onto the narrow log-and-dirt bridge straddling the steep gully, I saw that our rear wheel had plunged through the rotten timbers up to the axle.

Tib took the three kids back to solid ground. Gingerly, I jacked up the car, intending to fill the hole, then let the rear wheels back down and drive off. But searching that barren landscape produced nothing but small twigs and pebbles which fell right through the break in the bridge. Nowhere could we find rocks or logs big enough to plug the hole.

Since we had come to Africa we had never been in clearer need of guidance. We were still fifteen miles from the village where we planned to spend the night. Behind us were miles of empty bush; all afternoon we had met one car on the winding dirt track we were following in this little-traveled district of Uganda. Thunderclouds were building up over the Nile, and night would be upon us in half an hour. We couldn't spend the night in the car for fear the rest of the bridge would go. We couldn't stay out of the car: this was lion country. A mile back we had passed a fresh hippo carcass.

And so in this emergency we did what we had done frequently since arriving on this unpredictable continent. We asked God what to do. We used a principle we had used before, thanking Him ahead of time for the answer which we confidently expected would come. Then we simply waited.

And in the strange calm which follows this attitude, the answer was there, simple and perfect. I got out the spare tire, slipped it beneath the jacked-up wheel and found that it straddled the hole exactly. I let the car back down and, to the cheers of the children, drove off the bridge. Just in time too, for with nightfall came the first wave of a driving tropical rainstorm.

Now it would be possible, of course, to say that we had not received guidance at all, we were just using common sense. Once I would have been inclined to agree. But not today. For our African year, from beginning to end, was above all else an adventure in guidance. There where so much was strange, we found ourselves daily, hourly, sometimes minute-by-minute asking God's direction. And living like this month after month we discovered four principles that make His direction clearer to hear.

The first, which we used in the anxious moment on the bridge, is *thanksgiving before* guidance is received. There is something about a grateful heart that crowds out fear and quiets the mind to receive instructions.

A second principle which we found helping us again and again can be summed up in four words: pay attention to *coincidence*.

Among the many letters we wrote while planning the African year was one to Dr. Morton Hanna. I had known Dr. Hanna when I was a youngster growing up in Louisville; to me he was a name my parents mentioned more than a face. When Mother told us that Dr. Hanna was currently teaching at St. Paul's Seminary in Kenya, I naturally wrote him about the upcoming trip. Back came a letter from the school: Dr. Hanna was returning to Kentucky the month before our arrival. It seemed an indication that there was no role for us at this particular seminary and we dismissed it from our thoughts.

On our way to Africa we passed through Rome. Tib had wrung from the children a promise to sit wiggle-less through an evening at the opera there. It was summertime, though, not opera season. The only performance Tib could locate was in a tiny out-of-the-way theater in the suburbs. It was so small that we looked straight into the faces on the other side of the horseshoe-shaped balcony. And one of those faces was maddeningly familiar.

Since I'd fought in Italy during the war, I thought it must be someone I'd known then. Dusting off my all-but-forgotten Italian, I spoke to him during the intermission—and discovered that it was Dr. Morton Hanna, spending a few weeks in Rome on his way home from Kenya!

The more we thought about it, the more struck we were at the coincidence of this meeting, in this out-of-the-way theater, four thousand miles from the last address I'd had for him.

Next day we had lunch together while Dr. Hanna outlined the needs at St. Paul's Seminary: among them was a course in precisely the kind of down-to-earth religious writing *Guideposts* represents. In the end we did go to St. Paul's, for what turned out to be one of the most fascinating and fruitful of our African experiences.

At other times God's will was less apparent. That's when we relied on the principle of *opening and closing doors*. In one instance the door we needed to see swing open was a literal one: we needed a place to live. The choice narrowed to two cities with English-language schools for the children: Nairobi, capital of Kenya, at that time still a British colony, or Kampala, capital of newly independent Uganda. We'd been asked to work on Christian publications in both towns.

It seemed to us that the greater need was in Uganda, where teachers, missionaries, helpers of all kinds were in smaller supply. The problem—the door that seemed shut tight was housing. With embassy staffs pouring into the new capital, houses in Kampala were scarce and very expensive.

There was a missionary guest house in Kampala where newcomers could stay for one month. And so we asked, "Lord, if You mean us to stay in Uganda, open a way." We even specified where "our" house should be: in a local neighborhood among the people we'd come to work with, rather than the embassy enclave where foreigners congregated.

We started work at *New Day,* the Church of Uganda newspaper in Kampala. Daily we scanned the papers for house ads: nothing. We made the rounds of real estate agents; we even inquired at the American Embassy. Always nothing.

Twenty-five days passed. Twenty-eight. The time was at hand when we would have to leave the guest house, and Uganda. On the twenty-ninth day, we paid one final visit to the American Embassy. "Still nothing?" we asked. The officer shook his head.

"Nothing," he said. "Except, of course," he murmured as we turned toward the door, "that place out at Salaama."

What place? we asked eagerly. A house the Embassy itself had bought, he said, and then found that no one on the staff would live there. "It's way out in the boonies—no Europeans for miles around . . ."

We went to see it, and knew instantly that this was the door God had thrown wide. It sat on a hill overlooking Lake Victoria, and to New Yorkers accustomed to long commutes, the forty-five-minute drive into the *New Day* offices in Kampala seemed like living over the shop. We made a suggestion. The house was now standing empty. If the Embassy would let us have it for the *Guideposts'* budget, we'd act as caretakers.

On the morning of the thirtieth day we were called to the telephone at the guest house. The house was ours.

The fourth principle is the most mysterious of all: what we came to recognize as guidance in the form of a *nudge.*

113

In addition to our work as writers and writing teachers, Tib's personal prayer for the African year was to be able to teach in a setting where no European had taught before. By its very nature, of course, such a contact was going to be hard to make . . .

Five mornings a week we'd set out from Salaama in our small English-built Ford, taking the children to their English-language school in Kampala on our way to the newspaper office. When we first began this daily commute, we'd stop for the first hitchhiker who hailed us—but we soon learned why no one else did. With Liz on Tib's lap and the two boys squeezing together in back, we figured we could make room for three more—four or five if they were youngsters. But before we could shut the car door, seven, eight, nine people would have crammed joyfully inside, with others clambering onto the roof and even the hood, making further progress impossible.

So we were no longer doing this, when one afternoon, driving back to Salaama, our eyes were drawn to two teenagers, a boy and a girl, walking along the red-earth road in a group of perhaps a dozen.

To this day I cannot explain the impulse to stop and pick up this particular pair. "Shall we risk it?" I said to Tib, pointing out the two of them. She nodded, clearly as much at a loss as I was to explain the sense almost of inevitability about the idea. The sense of strangeness increased when not another youngster in the group even turned to look as we opened the car door—as though the automobile had somehow become invisible to any but those two.

They turned out to be brother and sister, and—again curiously—each time we came to a fork in the road they pointed to the route we ourselves were taking. When we reached the foot of our own hill I stopped the car. "This is as far as we go," I apologized. "I'm afraid you'll have to walk the rest of the way."

"But," said the boy in delightful English, "this rest of the way is accomplished." He pointed down a narrow track disappearing among the banana trees.

"I am Ddungu," he said proudly, "son of Muwanga, master of the school."

"School?" Tib and I said together. "We'd like to meet your father!"

Half an hour later we were being shown around a low mud-walled building by Muwanga himself, the first white visitors, he told us, his school had ever had. He had a hundred and fifty students, one other teacher besides himself. Yes, they tried to teach English—it had been voted the new nation's official language—but neither he nor his assistant spoke it well . . .

So began Tib's unforgettable nine-month teaching experience. It still seems remarkable to me that out of the hundreds of people trooping along that road out of Kampala, we should have stopped for the very two who held the answer to a prayer.

And in the years since, have we continued to need God's guidance? Of course. Daily, hourly, just as we did in Africa. We've come to believe that He has a perfect plan for each day—which the seeming routine-ness of familiar surroundings can lull us into overlooking.

We don't want that to happen. We want to remember to watch for the coincidence which, as someone has said, is "God's universe caught in the act of rhyming." We want to see opening and closing doors as His providence, rather than "luck" or frustration. We want to be responsive to impulses—provided of course that we can imagine Jesus yielding to them. They may be nudges from a wisdom beyond our own. Above all else we want to thank God ahead of time, knowing that although we see the pattern only dimly, it is there waiting for us in all its perfection.

John

Generation after generation, people have looked for counsel to the Bible. Are words written down in past millennia really valid for decision making today? How do we go about . . .

FINDING GUIDANCE IN THE BIBLE

In 1970 Tib and I faced a difficult decision: should we leave our staff positions at *Guideposts* in order to start a Christian book-publishing company? At stake were the jobs we'd held for twenty years, old friendships, deep loyalties, the use of time. We battled the question back and forth for weeks, but the pros and cons seemed equally weighted. It was an unsettled time and out of it—as so often out of difficult times—came some real discoveries about faith. Specifically, about the way God can use the Bible to guide us precisely at these crossroad moments.

One day in the midst of our uncertainty, we went to visit friends in upstate New York who had themselves recently faced an important decision. Scott and Nedra Ross had started a ministry to alienated young people, working out of an old barn near Ithaca. Hundreds of rootless kids had been helped, but by the end of the first year the Rosses were exhausted by the perpetual struggle to raise funds. "Do you think God's telling us to quit?" they wondered.

Scott and Nedra had heard of people seeking God's will by letting the Bible fall open at random, then reading the passage their finger lighted on. With some reluctance—it seemed a little like spiritual roulette—they decided to try it. An RSV Bible lay on the table. Nedra opened it, closed her eyes and put her finger down. The next moment she was reading these words from the eighth chapter of 2 Corinthians: "And in this matter I give my advice: it is best for you now to complete what a year ago you began . . ."

"That experience lifts us every time we think about it," Scott told us. "Maybe the Lord has something to say to you in the same way."

Well, like the Rosses, at first we were shy about the idea. We remembered Catherine Marshall's opinion-revealing term for the practice: Lucky Dipping.

But, with an attitude of "nothing ventured, nothing gained," we decided to try. As we drove along Route 17 enroute home from Ithaca, Tib took out a Bible, let it fall open and put her finger squarely on . . . the begats. "And Ozias begat Joatham; and Joatham begat Achaz; and Achaz begat Ezekias" (Matthew 1:9, KJV)

So much for Lucky Dipping. Obviously God does sometimes honor this way of seeking His mind. And, just as obviously, He wasn't doing it this time.

Weeks passed before our attention was drawn to a second way that God sometimes uses to communicate with His people: He plants in one person's mind a Bible verse intended as a message for somebody else.

Andy SoRelle is a wildcat oil driller. Over dinner in his

Texas home one evening he told us how he was flying his plane a few years ago over a stretch of wasteland near Houston when he thought he heard God whisper to him. *Do you see that fallen tree? Drill there and you will find oil.*

Andy was skeptical. And with reason, for he soon discovered that six major oil companies shared the mineral rights to that particular section, and every one of their geologists had come to the same negative conclusion. There was no oil there. Every company but one—Exxon—agreed to assign its rights to Andy. Exxon's automatic policy was to participate in such wildcat wells.

So Andy SoRelle, a little reluctantly, began drilling. Even the roughnecks—the men who work the oil rigs—shared the general lack of enthusiasm. At first Andy pretended not to notice the dubious glances that met him at the site. But as days stretched into weeks and costs soared past the $100,000 mark, his own doubts grew.

"There's nothing down there, SoRelle," the Exxon geologist concluded. "You can have our share if you want it." So now Andy had a hundred percent interest in a dry hole. If—that is—he wanted to go ahead.

It was a risky decision. Costs were running $2,000 a day, and now Andy would have to carry them alone. Soon he would run out of his own capital and have to start borrowing. Every day Andy asked the Lord what he should do.

Ray Hostutler is a rancher friend of Andy's in Corpus Christi, Texas. Ray did not know about Andy's new oil venture. Yet one morning while Andy was desperately seeking guidance, the phone rang at the SoRelles'.

"Andy?" It was Hostutler. "I believe the Lord's just given me a message for you. Read Isaiah 43, verses 18 and 19."

Andy hung up and turned quickly to the Isaiah reference. His heart began to race as he read the words. "Remember ye not the former things, neither consider the things of old," the passage ran. "Behold, I will do a new thing; now it shall spring forth; shall ye not know it? I will even make a way in the wilderness, and rivers in the desert."

The words that struck Andy strongest were, "Now it shall spring forth." Andy raced out to the well. The roughnecks were standing dejectedly about the pit. No one even said good morning. With a sinking heart Andy saw why: the mud in the pit was mixed now with hot salt water—to an oilman the worst possible sign. Andy felt sick. He turned his back on the well and walked away. Then, "SoRelle! Come here!"

Andy ran back to the pit. As he watched, the mud gave a little puff. Gas! Next came a film, a many-colored skim. Dumfounded, the crew stood at the edge of the pit and watched as the skim turned blacker. Oil! Cheering and shouting, the roughnecks and tool pushers and engineers and Andy thumped each other on the back. That well turned out to be a real producer.

For days after hearing this story Tib and I found ourselves waiting hopefully for the phone to ring. Or for someone at *Guideposts,* or someone at church, to say, "I have a Bible verse for you." But once again we were disappointed. Nothing of this sort happened. It didn't lessen our belief that God does speak in this way, but He didn't this time. So far, it seemed, we still did not have the key to being able to *count* on the Bible as a source of guidance.

Then one day we were in the kitchen talking with a friend, Co Holby, about our puzzlement. "I know," she said. Then she told us about an experience of her own that has made all the difference in the way we now look to the Bible for direction.

Co's husband Duncan had had a flare-up of an old heart ailment. Anxious and depressed, Co decided to see what comfort God might have for them in Scripture. She picked up a Bible, opened it at random and put her finger onto the page. "Do you know where it was?" Co said. "The Bible had fallen open to the page that separates the New and Old Testaments. There wasn't a thing printed on that page except the words 'The Gospel.'"

We were all laughing when suddenly my eye caught Tib's.

The gospel. Of course! That's where we should have been looking all along. When we asked the Lord to communicate with us through an individual verse tailored to our situation, we were actually asking for a little miracle. But we cannot summon up miracles; they come into our lives in a pattern all their own. The gospel, however, is a different matter. Through Jesus' life and teaching we could find encouragement and correction and all the counsel we needed.

At last we had what we'd been looking for. Together over the next few weeks Tib and I followed a program of reading the Gospels and holding up our decision to their illumination. Each morning we placed our surfacing emotions and motivations against Jesus' example. Were we afraid? Did we lack the faith to step out on our own? Were we greedy? Would a publishing company end up "serving Mammon"? How would our decision, either way, stack up against the priorities of His life?

And each day as we read, we saw the road before us a little more clearly. It happened to lead toward the new venture, but that was not the main thing to come out of those days. What has affected our lives even more is the principle of infusing our minds and emotions with the light of the gospel until—here a little, there a little—our decisions begin to reflect the decisions He has made before us.

John

*What was the strange nudging that led
an unsophisticated rural preacher to the
streets of New York City?*

TOO STRANGE TO
BE COINCIDENCE

One winter morning in 1958, a skinny country preacher named Dave Wilkerson was sitting in his living room, reading *Life* magazine. He turned a page and saw a picture of seven boys. That moment was to change his life.

Dave was pastor of the small Assemblies of God Church in Philipsburg, Pennsylvania. He felt at home in the slow-paced rural community; life for him, his wife and three small children was comfortably routine and it probably would have remained that way except for one thing. Dave Wilkerson had turned over his life to God. He had handed over his feet and his hands and his heart and asked the Holy Spirit to use them.

For Dave the Holy Spirit was no vague theological term; He was the Spirit of Christ, a living personality to be listened to and obeyed. On that particular morning, looking at the picture in the magazine, Dave Wilkerson began to weep.

The picture showed seven young defendants on trial in

New York City for the death of Michael Farmer, a young polio victim who had been brutally beaten by members of a teenage gang. Horrifying as it was, however, it was not the account of the murder which made Dave cry. It was the faces of the defendants. In their eyes he saw an anger and loneliness he had never known existed. All that day he was drawn to that picture. And as more days passed he felt the conviction growing that he himself—David Wilkerson—should take a toothbrush, get into his car, drive to New York where he had never been in his life, and try to help these boys.

At last Dave told his wife. "I don't understand why," he said, "but I must go." It was the boldest step of obedience to the Holy Spirit that he had yet taken. Almost before he knew how it happened, Dave and Miles Hoover, the youth director of his small church, were driving across the George Washington Bridge into New York City.

There he parked in front of a drugstore and telephoned the office of the District Attorney named in the article.

"No one can see the defendants," a clerk informed him, "unless the judge himself gives permission." But Dave's attempt to reach the judge by phone was unsuccessful.

So the next day David and Miles went to the trial: perhaps during a break in the proceedings they could present their request to the judge. All morning they sat in the visitors' section, eyes on the seven young defendants. As the court session closed, Dave popped to his feet, ran down the aisle and stood before the bench. If he was going to speak to the judge it would have to be now.

"Your honor? Would you do me the courtesy of talking with me for a few . . ."

"Get him out of here!" the judge ordered.

Two guards swept down on Dave, picked him up by his elbows and rushed him toward the rear of the courtroom. Reporters and photographers jumped to their feet, pleased to have some action at the end of the uneventful session. Flashbulbs popped.

Dave learned later that the judge had been threatened by gang members and had taken the skinny preacher for one of them.

That evening the newspapers carried stories about a Reverend David Wilkerson being ejected bodily from the courtroom. Dave and his youth director drove home to Philipsburg discouraged and confused. What kind of guidance had this been? In the Bible, men who were guided by the Holy Spirit effectively carried out God's will. David had simply made a fool of himself.

At home, he and Miles faced a disgruntled congregation, annoyed that their minister had made himself a public spectacle. As the days passed, Dave's confusion increased. Not only was it difficult to explain why he had gotten into such a mess; it was still more difficult to explain why, as soon as possible, he was going back to New York.

But that's where he was, the next week. When he telephoned the District Attorney's office a second time he was told that if he wanted to see the boys he needed written permission from each of the parents.

"Then," said Dave, "could you give me their names?"

The line went dead. In the phone booth Dave smoothed out the now crumpled page from *Life* and scanned the caption. The leader of the boys was named Luis Alvarez. To his dismay there were columns of Alvarezes in the telephone book. He started at the top.

In each case the answer was indignant. No, of course they didn't have a son Luis who was a defendant in the Farmer trial!

Dave was running out of dimes and there were still more than a hundred and fifty Alvarezes to go. He gave up and stepped outside, praying, "All right, Lord. I just don't know what to do next. If this is Your business I'm on, then Your Spirit will have to show me the way."

Dave got into his car and began to drive aimlessly through the strange streets. Eventually he found himself in the heart of Spanish Harlem. Tired of driving, he parked in the first empty space he found. He got out and asked a boy if he knew where a Luis Alvarez lived.

"Luis Alvarez?" said the boy. "You're parked in front of his house." He pointed to a brownstone building. "Fourth floor."

"Thank You, Lord," said Dave.

"What did you say?"

Dave put his hands on the boy's shoulder. "Thank you. Thank you *very* much."

Dave climbed to the fourth floor, found the Alvarezes' apartment and knocked on the door.

"Come in."

He pushed the door open and saw a tired-looking man

sitting in an overstuffed chair. Senor Alvarez barely looked up. "Ah, here you are, Preacher. I been expecting you. I see your picture in the paper. I say my prayers that you will come."

Early the next morning Dave was back at the city jail with seven written permissions to visit the seven boys on trial.

And here he was stopped definitively.

The jail chaplain, feeling that the boys were in his own spiritual care, refused to allow him entrance. David was crushed. "What are You trying to say to me, Lord?" he asked.

Dave had no way of knowing at that moment that this door had been closed in order for another—much larger—to open.

But in his prayer time back in Philipsburg the Holy Spirit began to speak to him. *Your vision was too small.* Perhaps God didn't intend him to minister just to seven boys but *to all the lonely, angry kids on the New York streets.*

Two weeks later Dave Wilkerson was back in New York. On this trip he brought with him no preconceived ideas of whom he was to help or how. He simply walked the streets, and everywhere he walked he made the same discovery: that photograph of him in a New York tabloid that had seemed to Dave like a mockery of his guidance was his entree to the street gangs of New York. Wherever he went he was recognized. "Hi ya, Preach!" from a cluster of kids on a street corner. "You're one of us, Davey!" from a tenement stoop. If the police jump on you, the thinking seemed to run, you must be on our side.

Soon the churches were asking questions about this man who was "in" where they'd never even had a toehold. Fifty parishes got together and asked him to conduct a two-week youth revival in St. Nicholas Arena. Five thousand teenagers flocked to hear him. A few months later Dave had a weekly television show where teenage dope addicts, adolescent alcoholics, and fourteen-year-old prostitutes told the stories of their conversions.

The following year Dave moved his family to New York to minister full time to these young people. At Teen Challenge Center in Brooklyn, hundreds of boys and girls in trouble found a new home and a new start. As for the seven defendants in the Michael Farmer trial, three were acquitted, four sent to prison where Dave's visits were welcomed by inmates and officials alike.

Meanwhile Teen Challenge centers had opened in Chicago, in Los Angeles, in major cities all around the country and the globe as World Challenge ministered Christ's healing love to alienated young people everywhere.

Amazing what can happen when an ordinary sort of man lets the Holy Spirit be his guide.

John

WITHOUT KNOWING WHY

Shirley and Terry Law tell their story to Elizabeth

SHIRLEY'S STORY:

The orange juice was poured, the oatmeal nearly cooked, and I was stirring the scrambled eggs, when the crazy thought popped into my mind.

Take the kids to breakfast at McDonald's.

At first I ignored it. I'd been warned by other young widows that your mind plays tricks on you, living alone. I hadn't exactly been alone since my husband's death in April 1984, six months earlier—but the children were only six and four.

Go to McDonald's.

The thought came more urgently, and for a second I wondered if I was cracking up. But surely the time for that would have been those two-and-a-half years of watching my tall, blond, athletic young husband die inch by inch of a brain tumor.

If grief hadn't been able to destroy my sanity, I told myself, mainly to keep my mind off this silly McDonald's notion, money worries might have. Jim had been a stock-broker here in Tulsa, Oklahoma, operating on commission, which stopped when he could no longer work.

I'd found a job selling Visa and Mastercard service to Tulsa businesses. It kept me out in the car a lot, and I'd cried a lot, there in the car, as Jim's condition worsened. If I'd been going to fall apart, that would surely have been the time, with everything seemingly against us. Even the washing machine broke down, with no money to repair it, so that in the evening after working and cooking and caring for Jim and mowing the lawn, I'd have to drive out to the laundromat.

Without faith in God, I thought as I gave the eggs a final turn, I really might have gone crazy. I'd carried a Bible in the car; when I felt panic rise I'd pull over and read until I could go on.

The oatmeal was ready. In the living room the kids were watching the Saturday morning cartoons. "Marie! Jason!" I called. "Wash your hands and come to the table."

And still something inside my head, quite independent of my own thoughts, was insisting that we were to leave this good hot meal right where it was, get in the car and drive a mile away to a fast food outlet. I'd never in my life eaten breakfast at McDonald's! Where could such a notion be coming from?

Where indeed . . . ? From the bathroom I heard Marie and Jason splashing water on the floor. I stood there at the stove, spatula in hand, thinking back to a chilly December day almost two years before. Wondering if the nudging in my head now was in any way like the nudging that had come to me then . . .

For a week I had been giving Jim and the children cold cereal because the stove, like the washing machine, had broken down, and Jim could no longer trust himself to try electrical repairs. We were three months behind on the house payments, and as for Christmas—Santa just wasn't going to find our chimney.

All that winter morning I had called on potential clients without success. As always when our situation threatened to overwhelm me, I'd pulled the car to the side of the road. And there God spoke to me as clearly as though He'd used audible words: *Will you trust Me, Shirley? For Jim, for the children, now and forever?*

I wanted to—oh, how I wanted to! But where could I get that kind of faith? Certainly I couldn't work it up on my own. "Father," I whispered, "give me that trust."

At once a kind of peace seemed to enter the car. And into that peace dropped the names of three local restaurants. I called on all of them that afternoon and signed on three new accounts.

From then on, these "impressions" came often, sometimes about work, sometimes about Jim's medication or about one of the children, until I learned to recognize them by a quality of loving urgency very unlike my ordinary thinking process.

This idea in my head now . . . If it had been anything except *go to McDonald's,* I would have said this was one of those times. But that was too ridiculous!

Wasn't it?

Marie and Jason scrambled into their chairs, still in pajamas on this one morning of the week when we could loaf around the house. Well, we could go to the drive-through window . . .

"Get your bathrobes on," I told them. "We're going to bring breakfast home from McDonald's."

"Yay!" shouted four-year-old Jason. "Can we get French fries?"

But Marie, two years older, looked from the waiting food to me, her face as bewildered as I felt.

Not the drive-through. Go inside to eat.

"On second thought," I called as the kids headed for their rooms, "let's put our clothes on and eat there."

"Boy," I heard Marie tell her brother, "does Mommy ever change her mind."

Twenty minutes later I was steering through Tulsa's Saturday traffic, as baffled as ever as to why we were doing this, when Marie burst into tears. "McDonald's makes me think of Daddy," she sobbed.

Jason was too young to remember the days when Jim could still drive and used to take the two of them out. But he wasn't too young to understand sorrow. "Don't cry, Marie," he said.

"Why don't we pray about it?" I suggested. So we did, and then Marie said, "God's going to give us a new daddy."

"Someone who loves God," added Jason.

I said nothing. Not out loud. But inwardly I was crying, *No!* No one could replace Jim. Not ever. It wasn't that I was mourning, exactly. I'd done that during the years of seizures and pain. Death had come as such a release for Jim that I'd had to release him too. It was just that I didn't want to open myself again to that kind of total involvement.

Before he died, Jim had asked me to remarry. "You're young, Shirley. You have your whole life ahead of you. Promise me you'll find someone else—when I'm gone."

But I don't want "someone else"! I protested inwardly as I pulled into the crowded McDonald's lot.

As I'd feared, on a Saturday morning there were long lines at the counter. Thinking ruefully of the eggs congealing in the skillet at home, I inched forward while the kids raced around the playground outside. At last I carried our trays to a window table.

That's where we were sitting when they came in, a stocky curly-haired man with a round, pleasant face— probably in his early forties—and three children, ages around twelve to five. I recognized the father at once: Terry Law, director of a singing group I'd seen on Oral Robert's TV program. Certainly no one I knew personally. And yet . . . the unmistakable "impression" came as I watched the four of them get into line at the counter:

This is the reason you are here.

These four people? This particular group, of all the parents and children jamming the restaurant at this moment?

I went on eating, but the food stuck in my throat. Two years' experience in trusting God was insisting, *Introduce yourself.* When I looked up they were setting their trays down at the very next table.

Lord, I objected silently, *he doesn't know me! I can't just say, "Hello, I'm Shirley."*

Then I remembered that a girl I'd known when I was growing up back in Portland, Oregon, had joined Terry Law's music group, Living Sound, several years ago. I could ask Mr. Law about Paula.

He seemed startled to have me speak to him. Paula had married a young man from Living Sound, he said, and together they were pastoring a church in Alaska. He was still looking at me oddly. Probably wondering why I was butting in on the one day he had with his family. More details about his work were coming back to me. Living Sound traveled all over the world, especially behind the Iron Curtain, where young people turned out by the thousands to hear contemporary music with a Christian message. He must hate to have strangers break into his precious time at home.

Just being polite, no doubt, he asked some questions too. When I'd come to Tulsa from Portland, what the kids' names were, what my husband did.

"Jim died last spring," I said. "I'm a widow." Mr. Law set down his coffee container so hard it slopped over. He mopped it up quickly, said he was sorry about Jim and wrote down my phone number to give to a lawyer he thought could be helpful in estate settling. Then with an apology he turned back to the youngsters who were clamoring for his attention.

What in the world, I wondered as Marie and Jason and I went out to our car, had flustered him so? And what, for that matter, I thought as I cleared away the cold remains of our uneaten breakfast at home, had this whole strange episode of dashing out to McDonald's been all about?

I wasn't really expecting God to tell me. I'd learned to trust Him these past two years, not to understand Him. The trusting is everything: it's peace and joy and security long before the answers come. We see only a step at a time, so He can't usually tell us why.

Except that, in this case, He did . . .

TERRY'S STORY:

The conversation with Don Moen occurred on a Monday. Don was music director of our organization, Living Sound, and as usual he and I were aboard an airplane. This particular September day in 1984 we were returning from Arizona to our base in Tulsa, Oklahoma.

Our "base"—that's how I thought of Tulsa now: the place we traveled from. Not "home," not since my wife Jan died, even though our three beautiful kids were there, and my mother, who'd come down from Canada to care for Misty and Scot and Rebecca.

Across the aisle of the airplane, Don was watching me. "It's two years this month, Terry," he said, as though reading my thoughts.

Two years since my world had changed in as long as it takes for a car to leave the road and crash into a ditch. I'd been far away in England when it happened. No one ever knew what caused the accident. Perhaps the afternoon sun was directly in Jan's eyes on that east-west Oklahoma road.

I only knew that my life seemed to have ended along with hers. I plunged into a bottomless despair, unable to pray or work or believe that I would ever do these things again.

It was in this mood that I went to see my friend and mentor Oral Roberts. Three months before I lost Jan, Oral had lost a son. "How do you keep going?" I asked him.

"I do it," he said, "by praising God."

Praise? When everything in me wanted to curse? "I didn't say feel it," Oral said. "It is simply a fact that God is very great. Tell Him so."

As Oral predicted, praise was the road back into life. Hollow and mechanical at first, it soon became genuine. Praise for Jan. For the thirteen years we'd had together. For her faith. For my knowing for sure that she was right now with Jesus.

Week by week the praise grew stronger—and so did my ability to do the things which at first had seemed impossible: to make plans, to travel, to minister to others around the world. Only the loneliness did not change. Praise helped me to live with the emptiness; it did not fill it.

Friends asked, of course, if I would consider marrying again. I knew I should, for the kids' sakes. Eleven, nine and four—how much they needed a mother!

I knew I should consider it for my mom's sake too. No one could have stepped in more selflessly than she had. But she'd raised her family. In justice she should be taking it easy now.

And yet . . . to consider marrying was just what I could not do. Every time I took my loneliness to God, He seemed to tell me: two years. It was always the same. I was not even to let the subject enter my head before that time. And that's what I'd told these friends.

Don was leaning across the narrow airplane aisle. "Two years," he repeated. "Remember what you said?"

"That I couldn't think about marrying for two years," I said. "And I haven't."

"Well, two years are up," Don persisted. "You'd better start thinking."

I leaned my head back in the seat, turning over my not-very-hopeful position. To me my three children were the greatest in the world, but what woman would want to take on marriage and motherhood all at once?

Where, for that matter, would I even meet an unmarried woman my own age? There were plenty of single girls in Living Sound, but they were kids in their twenties. I was forty-one. I'd want someone I could talk to. Someone who could understand the trauma that Misty and Scot and Rebecca had gone through.

I kept waiting for Don to pick up a magazine or something, but from the other side of the aisle he was regarding me expectantly.

"She'd have to be a widow," I heard myself say. "Someone who had as good a marriage as Jan and I had, and knows what it is to lose the most important person in your life. And," I finished, embarrassed at this outburst, "I don't know any widows."

"God does," Don said. "Let's pray about it."

"I will," I promised him, trying to close off a subject I wasn't ready for.

But Don had bowed his head. "Father, You know Terry's need, and his children's need. We believe You have a plan already at work . . ."

I glanced self-consciously at the other passengers. "Father," I joined in, keeping my voice as low as I could, "there's a widow somewhere who—"

"There's a widow in Tulsa," Don corrected.

"All right. In Tulsa. I ask that in Your own time—"

"Quickly."

"Okay. I ask that You quickly reveal . . ."

We prayed for several minutes, there on opposite sides of the aisle, I in generalities, Don in specifics. At the close, he stuck out his hand. With another nervous glance around, I reached across and gripped it.

"Thank You, Father," he pronounced, "that it's done."

Just like that. Prayer, in Don's view, didn't have to be long and eloquent. Just concrete and totally trusting.

At the office in Tulsa a number of crises were waiting for us. Living Sound had teams on the road both in the United States and Europe, including several Iron Curtain countries, and the week was unusually hectic.

Crises or no, however, Saturdays belonged to the family. This was the morning, when I was home, that I took the kids out to breakfast. And the outing always started with a debate.

"Grandy's," I suggested as we piled into the car, naming the place that made the pancakes I liked.

"Denny's," thirteen-year-old Misty voted.

"McDonald's," said six-year-old Rebecca.

"You just like the slide," Scot scoffed with just-turned-eleven sophistication. "I say Denny's."

"Denny's wins!" cried Misty.

"Now wait a minute, you two," I said. "Rebecca hasn't gotten to choose for weeks. Let's let her decide today."

And that was how, a few minutes later, the four of us were standing in the line at the McDonald's counter and I was gazing across the room at one of the most beautiful women I'd ever seen. Not a brunette beauty like Jan. This girl had hair the color of sunlight. In fact, where she sat at the window with two little tow-headed kids, the sun streaming through her long blond curls seemed to light up the room.

Maybe it was because I hadn't thought about marriage at all for two years, but I felt a stab of envy for her husband. I was thinking that it would be great just to sit near someone that pretty when, as we left the counter with our trays, the table next to hers opened up.

I was trying to decide how to strike up a conversation when to my surprise she did it for me: "Aren't you Terry Law?" A friend of hers, it turned out, had sung for a while with Living Sound. We talked about her friend and then about anything I could think of. I found out that her kids were named Marie and Jason. Their mother's voice was as nice to listen to as her face was to look at.

I peeled the lid from my coffee container as I thought up more questions. Like, "What does your husband do?"

When the girl with the golden hair said, "I'm a widow," I took a swallow that scalded my throat all the way down.

What else I said to her I can't remember, except that I managed to get her phone number with some excuse about a lawyer. All I could hear was Don Moen's prayer on the airplane only five days before.

All I could think was, *Oh, Lord my God, You are very great.*

Elizabeth

Postscript: Shirley and Terry were married in January, 1985, five months after the "chance" meeting at McDonald's. A sixth child, Laurie Ann, was born in March, 1986. "But she's not 'ours'," the Laws told me, "any more than all the rest."

E.

In the forty years since God led John and me—in spite of ourselves—into Christian writing, we've had a chance to learn about guidance from people who know it as a daily, hourly reality. Based on their experiences, here's a six-step experiment in . . .

LEARNING TO RECEIVE GOD'S GUIDANCE

STEP ONE: CHOOSE ONE AREA OF INDECISION THAT YOU WILL TURN OVER TO GOD.

For this experiment pick some situation currently perplexing you. Perhaps it's a business decision, a choice of schools or a place to live. Your area of indecision can be as important as choosing a marriage partner, or as minor as where you will spend your next vacation—but it should be something meaningful to you personally.

If the problem seems too self-centered to place before God: it's not. His way is always to meet us at our point of need, however mundane. Where He will lead us after this meeting is one of the wonderful discoveries of the life of guidance!

Remember though: with this decision, you are seeking the path that God has chosen—not trying to enlist His help in going your way. The guidance prayer is not: "Let Mary say yes," but: "Show me the partner You are giving me."

STEP TWO: ASK FOR GOD'S GUIDANCE.

Be specific! It helps to put the request in writing:

"Father, I want to be more aware of Your presence in my life. I acknowledge Your kingship over (name the general area: "my finances," "my time-use"). Today I am at a crossroads. I believe that at this moment there is one best decision I can make about (describe the specific situation) that will take me down the path You have prepared. Take me by the hand, Father, and lead me there."

Thank Him for the answer which He already sees in its entirety. Thank Him that in His perfect time He will reveal it to you.

STEP THREE: WATCH FOR HIS ANSWER.

Once you have phrased your request so that you know exactly what you are asking, and have prayed it through humbly and expectantly, you can assume that the process of guidance has already begun. Sometimes His answer will come quickly, other times not. The important thing is to be alert for His timing, not to insist on a schedule of your own.

It's important, too, not to be looking so steadily in one direction for your answer that you fail to see your guidance when it appears from another. We nearly made this mistake at *Guideposts* one time when we'd advertised for a new staff member. We prayed for guidance in choosing the right person among those who'd answered our ad. We were so busy evaluating these people that we almost missed the man God sent us, who walked in off the street with no introduction, no appointment, not even knowing that we were looking for a new employee—and became a valued editor.

What are some of the ways God reveals His guidance?

Verbally. God can speak through the "inner voice," through the words of the Bible, in words spoken in a prayer group, or even in the casual words of a friend who is God's mouthpiece at that moment. People use various expressions to describe the quality of such messages: "ring of truth" . . . "they spoke to my condition" . . . "I knew the words were for me." All carry the same implication: when God speaks to our intellect, He also speaks with a peculiar insistence to our heart.

Non-verbally. God can also lead in ways quite independent of words.

- Coincidence. The arrival in the mail of some unexpected money, the "chance" meeting of a friend, the odd recurrence of a certain theme everywhere you turn.
- Opening Doors. When you begin moving in a direction, do difficulties inexplicably dissolve before you, and solutions appear almost before you seek them? When God chooses your path, He walks it ahead of you.

■ Closing Doors. Conversely, if you find your progress blocked again and again, God may be telling you, "Not this way."

STEP FOUR: CONFIRM YOUR GUIDANCE.

Perhaps one of the above things has happened to you and you suspect it is guidance. How can you be sure?

Newspapers a few years ago carried the story of a man who built an ark, filled it with animals and waited in vain for the rains to fall. This poor soul had obviously encountered a sign of some kind; how can we be sure we too aren't deluding ourselves?

A good check is to wait until several forms of guidance coincide. Not only a Bible passage that seems apropos, but the same message in a letter from a friend, and furthermore obstacles vanishing when you act accordingly. God is not stingy with His guidance; He provides His signposts every way we turn.

One friend of ours, in his daily quiet time, habitually "hears" God give him instructions. When these involve major steps, however, he never acts upon them, or mentions them to anybody, until two fellow Christians independently make the same suggestion to him.

All along the path taken, too, guidance should be subjected to reconfirmation, to alteration or modification. E. Stanley Jones points out that divine guidance is not a searchlight illuminating the distant future but "a lamp unto my feet" (Psalm 119:105,

KJV). Only the step immediately ahead becomes visible. Seeking guidance is not a one-time affair, but a constant discipline, a training of the mind and heart in receptivity to God's will.

STEP FIVE: OBEY.

No matter how clearly we have perceived our guidance and how thoroughly confirmed it, nothing is accomplished until we act upon it. And yet, oddly enough, this is the area where guidance most often fails. As Moses could not grasp the fact that he had been singled out to lead the Israelites from Egypt, so you may find it hard to believe the directions God gives *you*.

Now is the time, as this experiment begins, to determine that you will act on whatever guidance God provides and confirms. Only in this way will you discover the power in this kind of prayer and lay a groundwork for further communication with Him.

STEP SIX: DISCOVER GOD'S PERFECT WILL.

Perhaps you began this experiment on a rather workaday level. God has higher purposes for you as well. True, He delights to lead us in every detail of our lives. The first guidance Jesus gave to Peter and his partners was in the area of their livelihood: He showed them where to cast their nets for a big catch. But this was only an introduction to the real work He had for them.

The same will be true of you. God loves you and will

continue to guide you in terms of your daily needs. But you can be sure that His perfect will for you, when you are ready to ask for it, will be to enlist you in the great and joyful work of His kingdom. Generations of Christians have found their over-all lifetime guidance in the Great Commission: "Go therefore and make disciples . . ." (Matthew 28:19, NKJV). This is His command to you, to me. How it will work out in detail in your life is the exciting living-out of daily, hourly guidance.

Elizabeth

PART FOUR

SEEING GOD WHERE THERE'S NEED

How can we see God more clearly? There's one sure way: uncover a need and there He will be, reaching out His hands in compassion.

His hands, of course, are our hands: He has no others on the earth today. The ears that hear the cry of need, the feet that run to help, are our ears, our feet. And as our ears and hands and feet respond, He opens our eyes to see His glory.

The Uninvolved
Could we join a church and keep our objectivity?

Letter from Shipboard
"How do you wage peace?" was our question. The seventy-eight-year-old man had an answer.

Thanksgiving at the Lake
"We can't sit here inside," said Liz, "while an animal's out there drowning!"

One Who Cared
Debbie was afraid of the dark city streets. The lighted subway looked like a safer place . . .

My Samaritan Experiment
A hundred cars passed us before someone stopped.

Johnny Elmseed
No one's too young to respond to need.

When Bob Sold the Paint Store
God didn't give reasons; all He said was: *Sell the store.*

The Skunk
If someone didn't do something the creature would die.

The Bridge on Route 59
At first we thought they were plastic bags, lying there on the sidewalk.

How to: Help When People Hurt
Finding where we fit with the need.

As journalists, we prized our objective viewpoint.

THE UNINVOLVED

It was 1959, the end of a long summer in the car. With our children, ages three, five, and eight, John and I had zigzagged twelve thousand miles across the country collecting stories for *Guideposts*. Occasionally, to the hypnotic hum of the tires, the children would fall asleep and John and I would have that rarity in the lives of young parents: time to talk.

It was in a flat stretch of North Dakota on the homeward leg that we got around to the subject of joining a church. In eight years of writing for *Guideposts* we'd interviewed people from every conceivable Christian background, finding strengths and truth in each. So much so that we could never settle on one denomination for ourselves. Indeed, our great advantage as religious reporters, we felt, was precisely our noninvolved status. As writers for an interfaith magazine we felt it gave us objectivity.

Now, as the children slept and the prairie stretched endlessly to the horizon, we wondered aloud if we paid a price for this reporters' stance. What if—just suppose—we started going to some church regularly, when we got home. Not sampling this one and that to get the "whole picture." Not as journalists. Just as ourselves.

Mentally we located the churches in our hometown. There was a handsome gray stone one, we seemed to recall, near the statue of the Indian chief who gave our town of Mt. Kisco, New York, its name. We didn't know what denomination it was, but . . . We'd be home for the start of school, just after Labor Day. We'd go to that stone church, we decided, until Thanksgiving.

I remember so clearly that rainy September Sunday when we drove into the parking lot, a sign informing us that we were at St. Mark's Episcopal Church. Inside the dimly lit sanctuary a central aisle led forward to an altar. And on the altar was a lighted cross, the only light in that large shadowy room.

Objectivity? that cross seemed to ask. *Noninvolvement?* "I don't know what it is to stand outside human life, looking on. My involvement with you on Calvary was total."

There must have been a sermon that day, and prayers, and hymns, but I remember only a lighted cross at the end of a central aisle.

More than thirty Thanksgivings have passed since then, and in all those years, except for travel, we have not missed a single Sunday at the stone church beside the Indian. Not because we find truth only there. Not that we have ceased to inquire of and learn from every believer we meet. Just that, in our eagerness to see God from many viewpoints, we had overlooked the view from inside.

Elizabeth

In 1962 Guideposts experimented with a new kind of involvement. John described how it came about in this . . .

LETTER FROM SHIPBOARD

August 10, 1962

To *Guideposts* readers:

I'm sitting in the writing room of the USS *Independence,* three days at sea. Tib and the children are seeing how far they can walk up and down the ship without retracing their steps, and I'm reflecting on what a difference a single conversation can make.

It began, of course, long before the conversation—it began in fact around the long conference table in *Guideposts'* office. For months we'd been meeting there to discuss the basic question of the nuclear age: "How do you wage peace?" Ideas had come slowly and I always left the table with a feeling that somehow I personally had not yet come to grips with the subject.

Then a year ago, in the summer of 1961, came an opportunity to interview Dr. Frank Laubach. This world-renowned literacy teacher had worked for fifty years in 101 different countries; he knew intimately the hopes and needs, the fears and ambitions of people all over the earth.

I talked with him for two hours one hot August afternoon just before this seventy-eight-year-old man took off on one more around-the-world literacy mission.

Dr. Laubach carries with him a large inflatable globe which he can blow up "in two minutes, thirty seconds, time me." Across large areas of the continents of Africa, Asia, India and South America, he has pasted a series of black stripes.

"Black," said Dr. Laubach, "to symbolize the darkness of ignorance, illness, hunger, misery." One half of the earth's surface, he showed me, lies in this darkness.

Then Dr. Laubach posed this question: "What are you people at *Guideposts* doing about it?" Before I could speak he went on, "There's a desperate need for a magazine like yours to get out and report on the heroic struggle these populations are waging. We need to focus the eyes of Christians in this country on the have-nots—because when an American sees a need, he'll seek out the solution."

Then Dr. Laubach leaned closer. "But reporting isn't all you could do. This nation is sending a whole army of compassionate men and women overseas. There's CARE, CROP, the Peace Corps, many others. There are specialists in farming, medicine, industry. I see you as part of this Army of Compassion, teaching *Guideposts'* kind of value-building journalism to the newly literate."

When someone learns to read, Dr. Laubach pointed out, he needs materials. Local materials, of importance to him personally. "What better to place in his hands than the kind of positive true-experience stories your magazine specializes in—but written by local people, about their own neighbors. Report and teach—that's what you can do to help tear off those black stripes. And when you do, you will have Christ with you because He told us, . . . *as you did it to one of the least of these My brethren, you did it to Me"* (Matthew 25:40, NKJV).

I left Dr. Laubach inspired by the sense of urgency that impels him. I wanted to rush home and repeat it all to Tib. She's an editor on the magazine, too, and a person who reads the morning paper as though it were a personal call to action.

I had a couple of stops on the way home, though: pick up a garden hose, drop off the snow tires to be recapped for the following winter. Somewhere between the garage and the hardware store, distant lands covered with black stripes ceased to seem real. Reality for us was Scott, age ten; Donn, age seven; and Elizabeth, age five. It was a house with peeling paint and an aging black cat. How could I account to Tib for the strange feeling that some unglimpsed portion of the earth was also our affair?

"Well," I said to myself as I turned into the driveway, "I'll just tell about it as though it were any other interview. I'll tell it flat—and watch to see if she feels anything."

And so we took a walk down Hog Hill Road, where we always go when we want to speak consecutive sentences to each other. Tib remembers my flat, dispassionate presentation as a rather bad job of acting. She stopped me finally and looked me in the eye. "You signed up, of course," she said. And from that moment, we were on our way.

We presented the idea to *Guideposts* the following week and there was immediate enthusiasm. Discussions were held, costs figured. The question arose: if *Guideposts* were to send Tib and me to some Third World area for a year, where on the globe would the time be best spent?

Over the next several months we wrote letters to people all over the world asking this question. Again and again the answer came back: Africa. Especially East Africa, where independence is coming so swiftly on such a narrow base of history. People there are stepping into the space age who eighty years ago had never seen a wheel, a written word or a number system. Apparently the balance between responsibility and chaos, plenty and starvation, was so precarious in this area that even two people, even in a single year, could make a difference.

Africa! Tib and I rushed to a map with such profound questions as, is Uganda the capital of Kampala, or the other way around? And, where is Tanganyika? Tib bought a phrase book in Swahili, the lingua franca of the area, and soon the children were saying *chumyi* and *pili pili* at the supper table for salt and pepper, and relishing the fact that *kiti* was not the cat but the chair they sat on.

Some of the phrases in the book did give us pause: "The darkness has prevented my seeing the snake," and "The lion has frightened the children." And when we found in the vocabulary at the back no word for "automobile" and seven different words for "ant," the shape of Africa was suddenly drawn for us more vividly than on a map.

To say that these discoveries throttled our enthusiasm,

though, would not be true. The sense of excitement grew steadily as we began to receive invitations from Tanganyika (south of Kenya), Kenya (north of Tanganyika), and other countries: invitations to teach journalism at several universities, to write books for new literates, to join the staff of a struggling newspaper. We accepted as many as we could.

Our excitement was not even dampened last spring when we began a series of fifteen injections against diseases I supposed had gone out with the Middle Ages. ("If this is traveling," said Donn as he bared one arm for typhus, the other for cholera, "I like staying home.")

By early summer our itinerary was booked: to Naples by boat, then by air to Beirut, Jerusalem, Cairo, Nairobi, Kampala—capital of Uganda, of course!—place names that would soon have streets and faces for us.

And so, nearly a year after my interview with Dr. Laubach, we were ready to go. Except for one problem that seemed to have no solution: what to do with the cat. But one day, shortly before the sailing date, the man who is renting our house came out to take some photographs for his wife who was still in Holland. Into the range finder strolled the cat.

"So like my wife's cat!" he cried. "She will be so sad to leave him when she comes to America. I don't suppose you would consider leaving yours with us . . ."

To the children this meant we could leave.

Three days ago we waved good-by to our friends from *Guideposts* and sailed out of New York harbor, feeling that God's hand was indeed on every detail of this year. What the months ahead will bring He alone knows. One thing we do know: wherever the Army of Compassion goes, its Leader has gone ahead, long before.

John

What if the need is too complex for us to tackle?

THANKSGIVING AT THE LAKE

At first the thin ice seemed no more than a disappointment. Each year our family gathers for Thanksgiving at a lakeside cabin in the Catskill Mountains. It's deer season with the woods full of hunters, so our activities are confined to the lake: skating and ice-fishing if it's frozen over, fishing from the canoe if it's not.

It certainly looked frozen as John and I climbed from our car. It wasn't, though. Just an inch or so of ice, too thick to use the canoe, not solid enough to walk on.

The unusable lake was forgotten in the excitement of new arrivals. Nine of us were there that year. Three from my sister's family. Our daughter Liz and her husband. Our son Donn and his wife. John and I. Cooking in the small cabin takes coordination: the turkey went into the oven at once, the pies would have to wait until the bird came out. Meanwhile there were vegetables to peel, the tablecloth to get from the mouseproof chest.

By two o'clock the aroma of roasting turkey was evoking Thanksgiving images. The other cabins around the lake were shuttered and silent. Except for an occasional distant rifle shot we were alone in the woods; it was not hard to imagine a solemn file of pilgrims emerging between the trees.

I was making celery curls when we heard it, a brittle tapping from somewhere outside.

"A deer! Look—on the lake!"

All of us rushed to the window. There she was, a slender doe running across the ice. As we stared, her hooves went out from under her on the slippery surface. In an instant she had scrambled back to her feet. We hurried out onto the porch to see better. "She's running from hunters," Liz guessed. Again and again the doe fell, struggled up, plunged on, driven by some unseen terror at her back.

She had reached the middle of the lake when she fell once more. But this time instead of a thud there was a splash as the thin ice gave way beneath her.

The doe's head reappeared above the water. She flung her front legs up on the ice and thrashed with her hind ones, trying to climb out of the hole formed when she fell. For a full minute the surface churned. At last she let her forelegs slide back into the water—only to hurl herself again at the ice a moment later.

We ran down to the water's edge to test what we knew already. Donn took a few steps onto the ice, crashed through into two feet of water and splashed back to shore. While he dried off by the Franklin stove, the rest of us tried in vain to force open a channel with the canoe. Each time the water in the center of the lake began to fly, so did ideas and counter-ideas: "If we could just get a rope around her!" ("But how do we get to her?")

I grew chilled and went back inside to watch from the window, muscles straining with the deer's. Donn's wife, Lorraine, came up from the silent vigil at the shore: "She can't last long in that cold water."

But a swift death was denied the struggling creature too. As the afternoon shadows stretched across the lake, the pathetic flurries of kicking continued. The cold had driven the last of us inside, but the tragedy taking place beyond the window set the mood of our conversation. My sister's husband, Alan, a Third World economist, foresaw widespread starvation. Donn, who sells medical equipment in South America, spoke of the health crisis there. Liz described the growing need and dwindling resources in her field of social work. The hopeless effort of the deer was like the hopelessness we all felt in the face of problems too complex to have answers.

By the time the turkey was ready, giving thanks was the last thing any of us felt like. I put the pies in the oven. Less often now, but still with heartbreaking determination, came the clatter of forehooves on the ice.

Liz placed the rolls in a baking pan. On the stove the gravy was thickening. From the lake came a flutter of kicks.

And with that, Liz jerked off her apron. "We can't!" she cried, her stricken face reminding me of the little girl who used to bring home hurt birds and ailing kittens. "We can't sit in here eating Thanksgiving dinner while an animal's out there drowning!"

The moment she said it, there was a rush for jackets and mittens. We didn't know what we were going to do, but we had to do something. I turned the oven to "low"—heaven knew what the pies would turn out like—and followed the others out the door.

A quarter mile away as we circled the lake, we came upon a rowboat lying bottom up on the shore. Sturdier than the canoe, perhaps it could ram its way through. We got it upright and down the bank, where it crashed through the ice and wedged tight.

"Rocks!" someone suggested.

We scattered into the woods and staggered back with the largest stones we could carry, passing them to those in the boat who hurled them onto the ice beyond the bow. Most simply skittered away, a few made small holes, nothing a boat could force its way through. Already on this short November day the sun was setting. Her hours of beating at the ice had opened a considerable circle around the deer in the center of the lake. Her head, motionless now, showed above the rim of ice, half a football field away.

"A pickax!" But we didn't have a pickax.

"We do have a sledgehammer," my nephew Doug recalled. He raced back to the cabin for it, and in a few moments the men in the family were spelling each other, standing in the bow battering at the ice while another fishtailed with the canoe paddle at the rear. It took several blows to make a foot of progress as the hammer stuck, was wrenched free, stuck again. Slowly, so slowly, the boat inched forward into the narrow channel opened by the hammer.

Too slowly. After twenty minutes of furious battering, the boat had traveled ten feet.

On the shore we were stamping our feet on the frozen ground. Soon it would be dark. We had tried . . . and failed.

And then Liz's husband, another Alan, had an idea. "If we tied a piece of rope to the handle," he said, "maybe when the sledgehammer sticks we could haul the boat toward it."

There was another dash to the cabin. The two Alans climbed back into the boat. And now for the first time there was movement. On a good lob the hammer would stick fast; pulling on the rope, men and boat would slide up onto the ice, where the weight would crash through, not inches but whole yards at once. Instead of hoping for a swift death for the suffering animal, we began to pray that she could hold out until they reached her.

But in fact the deer was very much alive. Alive and thrashing in terror, as with flying hammer and straining men the rescue craft drew near. From the shore we saw the boat break through into the hole the deer had made.

And now what? We shouted advice in plenty, but getting a rope around the neck of a panic-stricken animal proved out of the question.

"Get behind her!" Doug called. That too was simpler to say than do, but swiveling the boat with the paddle they gradually herded the frightened creature toward the channel they had opened from the shore. Unwittingly, propelled by fear of the boat behind her, the deer swam toward land.

"Hide!" we cautioned one another: she mustn't see us. We faded back among the trees. Legs folded beneath her, the deer coasted into the shallows. She could touch bottom easily now and stand.

But she did not. She floated slowly into shore and huddled there. We could see her large wary eyes, her heaving sides.

Still she did not straighten her legs. It had never occurred to us that she might have broken them, or gashed her chest against the sharp-edged ice. Concealed by the trees, not daring to talk for fear of adding to her stress, we could only watch in silence.

Slowly the liquid eyes closed, the long, sensitive face dropped until the chin was resting on the bank. She was not dead, for her eyes would open from time to time, but it was clear to us all that she was dying. Even when the two Alans brought the boat up to her flanks and stepped across her, she did not move.

The nine of us walked a few more paces away among the trees and held a council of despair. An injured doe bleeding to death there at the water's edge, or freezing to death as the night and the ice closed in—it was unthinkable. We were hungry, discouraged, chilled to the bone, yet unable to desert a dying animal here in the woods.

A splashing of water turned every head to the lake.

The "dying animal" had sprung to her feet. For an astonished moment we stared at her in the twilight—larger, taller than we imagined. Then in three arching leaps she was gone, bounding between the trees and out of sight before the cheers had left our throats.

We ran to the water's edge: no trace of blood where the doe had lain. Only the spot where the exhausted animal had paused to collect her strength.

We were ridiculously elated, frozen feet forgotten as we tramped back to the cabin singing "Come, ye thankful people, come!" at the top of our voices. The deer had escaped into a world full of peril and problems. A hunter could shoot her tomorrow. She could get hit by a car on the highway or starve to death over the winter. Such things were beyond our ken.

The turkey was cold, of course, by the time we sat down, and the pecan pie had to be poured rather than cut. But the thanksgiving was from our hearts:

"Thank You, Father, that in this complex world You have given each of us some small part to play."

Elizabeth

Her screams rang through the subway.
Nobody responded until the arrival of . . .

ONE WHO CARED

The boys had been drinking. Arms locked, they marched in threes and fours—a dozen or more of them—through the streets of downtown Philadelphia. They had a plan in mind; they were going to crash the Saturday night dance at a local hotel because they lacked ticket money. They were dressed for the occasion. Beneath topcoats they wore neatly pressed suits and ties, their shoes were shined. The oldest of the boys was eighteen, the youngest thirteen.

The ticket taker at the dance remembered them, remembered that they used vulgar language when she told them they could not come in. The boys withdrew to a corner of the hotel lobby, huddled, then advanced toward the ballroom door. There they were stopped again, this time by a man who was big enough to scare them. They left swearing revenge. In the all-but-deserted street outside, they met four boys coming to the dance. They jumped the newcomers and knocked them to the sidewalk. Laughing, the gang marched away.

Another person who remembered them was the cashier at the change window in the Vine and Race Street subway station. She heard the boys run down the stairs behind her, and she saw them jump the turnstile and scurry down the second flight of stairs to the subway platform.

Below, on the passenger platform, six men carrying bowling balls were waiting for a train. The boys looked them over.

"Hey, Dad! What time is it?"

"Ten o'clock."

The gang moved down the platform, out of sight of the men behind the wide green-and-white tiled pillars that support the subway ceiling. A short while later there was a sound of a bottle crashing against the tracks.

Fifteen minutes earlier and two blocks away, a sixteen-year-old girl, Debbie, pocketed her baby-sitting money and stepped out into the streets.

Debbie was not from Philadelphia and the city streets at night made her nervous. The cousin she was visiting had gotten a date for that evening at the last minute, and Debbie had taken her baby-sitting job. Now the dark empty sidewalk frightened her. She was glad when she reached the lighted subway stairs.

She dropped a coin in the turnstile, pushed her way through and went down the second flight of steps onto the subway platform. A group of men stood chatting at the north end. Instinctively she edged away from them and wandered south down the platform until they were out of sight behind the pillars.

A noise came from the tracks: it sounded like a bottle breaking.

Debbie stopped. From behind a pillar a heavyset young man appeared, moving toward her. Debbie backed away.

Now she could see a whole gang of boys behind him. The first one said something but a rush of air whistled up the subway tracks and she could not hear. If only the train would come. And then suddenly the first boy grabbed her arm and pulled her to him. Debbie smelled alcohol. She screamed and his hand went over her mouth. Another boy grabbed her dress: she heard it tear. She bit the hand at her mouth and screamed again. The men at the other end of the platform! Why didn't they come!

Perhaps half an hour before Debbie entered the subway station, a twenty-three-year-old college student from Chamblee, Georgia, James R. George, bought a second cup of coffee at the cafeteria where he'd just finished his dinner. A Naval Air Reservist, "Bud" George was spending his spring vacation at a training session in antisubmarine warfare at Willow Grove Naval Air Station outside Philadelphia. It was his first trip north; he'd spent the afternoon visiting historic sites.

"Kind of funny," he mused. "Here I am with a weekend pass in my pocket, and what do I do for fun? I go to Independence Hall."

Bud's parents had had one simple method of bringing up children. They raised them on the Bible. Every evening Mrs. George would assemble the children and methodically, a chapter a night, read straight through the Bible. She was not reading to entertain; she was reading to train. The children were often bored, but other times their eyes glistened at the stories of Daniel, Joseph,

David—stories of men responding heroically to the situations which God presented to them.

Bud finished his coffee and left. He passed the Vine and Race Street subway station. It was ten past ten: getting late. Maybe he'd go back to Willow Grove and save a hotel bill.

Bud did not come into the station by the main entrance but by a secondary entrance at the south end where there's an automatic turnstile. He put his money in the slot, pushed through and went down to the platform.

At the other end a group of men carrying bowling balls were peering curiously down the track in his direction. Nearby he could hear scuffles and laughter.

"Teenagers cutting up," he thought.

And then he heard a scream.

"Let me alone!"

Bud ran toward the sound. Suddenly, around the column, he came upon a scene so unbelievable that for a minute he could only mistrust his eyes. There, out on the open subway platform—with several men standing within earshot and a train rumbling down on them—a group of boys were holding a screaming, nearly naked girl on her back.

Several of the boys saw him and jumped up. "Get that guy!"

Bud swung and hit the first one in the mouth. He felt a blow in his stomach and missed his next punch.

A headlight appeared down the track. Four of the boys were dragging the girl out of sight beneath the stairway.

A fist crashed into Bud's nose and blood spurted. The train screamed into the station. The group of men who had been waiting quietly stepped aboard.

Another fist hit Bud in the eye as he felt his own slam into bone. Then he got a rabbit punch in the back of the neck. Someone was kicking him with sharp-toed dancing shoes. He does not remember climbing the stairs, only crawling up the last one, shouting to the cashier in the subway change booth.

"Call the police! They're attacking a girl!"

The cashier picked up her telephone and dialed the number. Bud went back down the stairs, steadying himself on the railing. Far down the tunnel the red taillights of the train receded into the distance. A police siren wailed in the street above. The boys jumped onto the tracks and started running. In what seemed like seconds the station swarmed with police; several ran down the tracks after the boys, one gave Bud first aid, another went to help the girl.

An officer came down the platform, his coat around the hysterical girl. "Let's get you two to a hospital."

Above, a row of police cars waited, red lights whirling. The police put the girl in one, Bud into another, and sped them away.

When the doctors had treated Bud's injuries, they let him inquire about the girl. She had been badly beaten and one of her teeth knocked out, but Bud had reached her in time to prevent a rape. Within twenty-four hours all of the boys involved had been arrested. Bud testified at the trial: most were sentenced to a correctional institution.

And Bud found to his amazement that he was a celebrity. Newspapers, radio, TV, everyone wanted to interview him.

"Where did you get the guts?" one reporter asked him. "From the things we read today, people don't want to get involved."

Bud thought a minute. He thought of his parents' living room in Georgia, and the Book that was always open . . .

"It depends," said Bud, "on what you read."

John

This time we were the ones in need . . .

MY SAMARITAN EXPERIMENT

One hot afternoon several years ago Tib and I were driving along a lonely stretch of I-75 in south Florida when a dashboard warning light began to glow—a red square with a picture of a watering can on it. I stopped the car on the side of the road and opened the hood.

And that was the beginning of an unexpected adventure—an experiment in following the Good Samaritan.

I stared down into the steaming engine. I'm no mechanic but I could see what the trouble was: the wheel that drives the fan belt had somehow flown apart.

Tib got out too, and we stood in the glare of the August sun, looking down the empty stretch of highway. A car appeared, traveling fast. It passed without slowing down. In a minute or two, another car; that driver didn't even glance at us. I tried to remember what the last big green overhead sign had said . . . I knew the figure was "40 miles." How far had we come since then? Even a few miles would be too far to walk in this heat, and if I tried to drive, the motor would melt.

So all we could do was stand on the sun-browned verge and "wait for patrol" as signs along the highway had advised. I couldn't remember seeing even one patrol car since we got on the interstate. A livestock truck went by, then a cluster of cars. The drivers were apparently in too big a hurry to stop—or possibly they were afraid to. A rash of highway robberies had recently made headlines in southern Florida. But how dangerous did we look! A balding man in his sixties, a woman a few years younger. In any event we stood beside our automobile as ten, twenty, forty cars passed. I stopped counting an hour and a half later at one hundred.

Finally, a muddy pickup slowed as it passed us, right-turn light blinking. I ran forward as it pulled onto the shoulder. The driver, probably in his thirties, wore a yellow cap with the word "Caterpillar" on it. His overalls were caked with gray mud.

"*Problemas?*" the young farmer asked. He turned out to speak about as much English as I do Spanish, which is to say not much.

"Cooling system's shot," I said, indicating with a circular gesture that my fan belt was broken. The man walked back to our car, looked under the hood and shook his head. With his own sign language—pointing to us, then to his truck, extending both arms as if steering a wheel—he told us clearly enough that he'd take us to find help. So we locked the car and got into the cab of the truck. To see out the mud-splattered windshield from my spot in the middle, I had to look past a crucifix dangling from the mirror.

The farmer took the first exit, twenty miles down the road. It was another five miles to the nearest town. At the garage, he waited long enough to be sure we were being looked after, then headed for his truck. I followed, pulling out my wallet in an awkward offer to pay him for his trouble. He shook his head no. So we simply shook hands and he was gone.

It took the garage several hours to locate a suitable part but before nightfall we were on our way, still giving thanks for our Good Samaritan. "How do you repay a kindness like that?" I said to Tib.

"We can't," she said, "but maybe we can pass it along."

Pass it along! Of course—there was my answer. "I'm making myself a promise," I said to Tib. "I'm going to stop and help another driver stuck on a highway somewhere." I paused. That seemed so little. "No, not *one* other driver," I said. "I'm going to help ten!"

Forming that high-minded resolve was one thing; acting on it was another. The very next day after our own rescue we saw a stalled car and I slowed down—until I spotted the man inside wearing studded black leather. I kept going. I probably misjudged the poor guy, but still there *are* angry and deranged people out there. Clearly, there had to be a certain rightness about stopping. That's a judgment call, so I asked God to guide me.

Then, too, like most people I always seem to be in a hurry. The next few times I saw a car stopped beside the road, it happened that someone was waiting for me—so again I did not stop. Perhaps it was just an excuse, but I told myself that it wasn't fair to pass the time-cost on to someone else.

Even with these bumbling false starts, however, I did

find plenty of occasions when I could assist someone. Tib's and my work as writers keeps us on the move, and she was with me on the very first Samaritan adventure. We were driving through rural New Jersey when we passed a late model Lincoln stopped beside the road with a family gathered around it—a man, a woman and two youngsters—both the father and the little boy wearing yarmulkes.

Tib and I exchanged nods.

The embarrassed man told us they'd run out of gas. We opened the back door and the father got in. As we drove to the nearest filling station we told him the story of the Good Samaritan who had stopped for us in Florida.

That night Tib and I were unpacking the car back home in New York, when on the floor of the backseat we found a wallet. It could only belong to the man we had stopped for. Inside was his identification: he was an anesthesiologist from Trenton. We reached him by phone, told him we'd found his wallet and would send it by certified mail in the morning.

"Hope you weren't worried," I said.

"Of course not. Would the Good Samaritan steal?"

Since then I have stopped for breakdowns in half a dozen states, as well as in Canada, Mexico and Europe.

Being a Good Samaritan has sometimes involved more than just driving a few miles out of the way. Sometimes it has required a small expense—a couple of dollars for phone calls or a cup of coffee. One day I was driving through the outskirts of Charleston, South Carolina, when I passed a truck filled with fresh produce stalled at curbside with its hood raised. A block farther I noticed a grizzled man about my age trudging down the road lugging what looked like a heavy auto part. I pulled over. "That your truck back there?"

The stubble-bearded man put down his load. It sure was! "This confounded starter motor again! If you can take me to the parts yard . . ."

As it turned out, the man was short just a few dollars of the price of the replacement part. A very few—nothing like the size of the smile that warmed me on my way after I'd driven the man back to his truck.

Sometimes stopping costs time. Barreling along a California freeway one winter day I passed an old Pinto on the edge of the highway, flying the universal signal of distress, a handkerchief tied to the radio antenna. A woman sat in the driver's seat.

By the time I'd sized up the situation, I was perhaps a quarter mile away with no place to pull over. I'd have to exit, reverse directions, get off again in order to get back to her. The round trip took twenty minutes, during which time I was sure someone else would have stopped. But no, she was still there, and she was crying.

"Don't mind me," she apologized. "I've been sitting here over an hour. Even the police didn't stop."

I took extra time with this lady, waiting with her at a drive-in restaurant until the road-service people arrived. Over coffee I told her about our Florida experience. "Thank God for that farmer," she said as the tow truck pulled in. "Because of him you're here today."

It's true. Because of that farmer, a minor chain reaction of kindness has started. About three months after this adventure began Tib and I were driving along a levee above the Mississippi River when we came upon a young black woman in a battered station wagon full of children. We pulled alongside and asked if she was having car trouble.

Indeed she was. They'd stopped to eat lunch and now her car wouldn't start. With our jump cable I got her engine going. "How much?" she asked, opening a worn brown handbag. In answer I told her about the farmer who had stopped for us.

"I'm going to do it!" she exclaimed. "I'm going to help out ten people just like you're doing!"

This young mother's reaction to my story of the Florida Samaritan was typical. People often promise to pass his thoughtfulness along. Some admit they'd be too timid to stop along a highway, but say they'll find another way to help, such as calling the highway patrol at the next exit.

I am glad others want to keep the Samaritan chain intact. I believe they'll find, as I have done, that the rewards far outweigh the minor inconveniences. Some responses are touching. One skinny boy with a huge radio, which he kept at full volume throughout our drive to a motorcycle shop, shouted that he couldn't believe someone old enough to be his *father* had stopped to help him.

But for me the biggest reward has been a shift in my own attitudes. Over the years I'd let myself become a bit suspicious of strangers, people of another race, another generation or culture. It's well to be sensible, of course;

we do live in a century of violence (as did the biblical Good Samaritan). But I am not going to let fear play a larger-than-life role for me. Most people are friendly, most are honest, and I want to side with those—like the Samaritan in the dirt-splattered pickup who stopped to help us—who act on this assumption.

It has been more than three years since I pulled over for my first motorist-in-need. During this time I've met tourists from Japan, businessmen, a rodeo clown, several students, a Jamaican migrant worker. My tenth stop has long since been completed. But by now I'm enjoying these encounters so much that I wouldn't stop stopping for the world!

John

Can one person do anything for our endangered planet? Even a twelve-year-old boy from a rural town in Maine?

JOHNNY ELMSEED

Back in 1983 twelve-year-old Shawn McNutt was looking for a project he could undertake. A dedicated Boy Scout, Shawn had made it all the way to Life rank; now he aimed at the top in Scouting, Eagle. To achieve that goal he needed to complete a community service project. What he didn't know that wintry morning when he walked into his junior high class in Sebago Lake, Maine, was that the project he would find would have an effect all across America.

Shawn had a test in social studies that day. His teacher told the class that anyone finishing early could read the latest issue of *Current Events,* a newspaper written for young people. Shawn turned in the exam and picked up a copy of the paper. In it was a picture of a man cutting down a huge, dead elm.

The elm, America's favorite shade tree . . . The year before, when Shawn was working on his Forestry merit badge, his dad had told him that there used to be a dozen elms right in their own yard. All that was left was one old stump, too tough to rot.

"We cut those trees down the year you were born,

Shawn," his father had said. A blight had wiped out most of the elms in Sebago Lake, and in the rest of New England too.

The blight had been caused by a fungus brought into the country on lumbering logs imported from Holland half a century ago. Until recently, the *Current Events* article said, there wasn't much anyone could do about trees attacked by Dutch elm disease except cut them down and burn them. But today there was hope. A nonprofit organization in Harrisville, New Hampshire, called ERI, the Elm Research Institute, was working to help the elm tree. "And," the article went on, "you can help, too."

Shawn read on. The article said you could assist elms in two ways: you could locate living trees and inject them with a fungicide, and you could plant seedlings of a new variety resistant to the blight. Anyone spotting a large, living American elm and sending the location to ERI for possible treatment, the article concluded, "will receive a free elm seedling to plant."

The school bell finally rang, and in half an hour Shawn was running into his own almost treeless yard carrying the copy of *Current Events*. While his mother set out cookies, Shawn told her about his idea for his Eagle project. His mother caught his enthusiasm, and that was important. The undertaking would involve the whole family.

That night Shawn told the others. His dad said he'd drive Shawn around to spot elms, and his little sister, Lynn, said she'd help keep records.

Scouting authorities approved the project. The original Boy Scout concept of service to God and man was still central to the spirit of Scouting. What better way to serve man than to save these graceful symbols of small-town America, and what better way to serve God than to become involved in the stewardship of His creation.

From the ERI Shawn got a quick answer. If he'd take a census of all living elm trees in his area at least six feet in circumference, giving the trees' location and the names of the property owners, the Institute would send him two seedlings for every tree he listed.

Shawn and his dad started crisscrossing the region. "I knew my dad would help," Shawn says. "The time when I was working on my Hiking merit badge, I asked Dad if he'd walk with me to church. Dad said of course he would. But our church happens to be twenty-two miles from home. We got up at four in the morning and when we got to church I was so tired I fell asleep during the sermon."

They'd start in the late afternoon when his father got home from his job at the paper mill. There weren't so many big elms left in Sebago Lake, so the McNutts had to range a bit. But just about everyone was glad to help.

"Son," one man said, "that old tree's been on this farm for a hundred and fifty years. Anything you can do to help it, you got me behind you."

It took three weeks to take the census and more time for Shawn and Lynn to check ownership records at town hall, but at last Shawn sent his results off to ERI. Back came the response: a manila envelope with Shawn's name on it. That night, with the whole family standing around, he opened the package on the kitchen table.

"Out fell a snarl of seventy of the tiniest trees I'd ever seen," Shawn says. "Just sprouts, really, thin little brown things with buds at the top where leaves would be."

Next day Shawn took the seedlings out to his mother's garden and dug seventy cup-sized holes a few inches apart, making a mud soup of the soil for a planting mix. He contacted the people he'd met during the canvass and asked them when they'd like a little blight-resistant tree planted on their property.

And so it was that after months of diligent work, Shawn McNutt became an Eagle Scout.

But the story doesn't end there. In 1985 at the great Boy Scout Jamboree in Virginia, Shawn learned that the project he had started as a personal venture had become a national Scout undertaking. Today thousands of trees are waiting in flats at the research center in New Hampshire. These seedlings are even better than the ones Shawn planted; developed by researchers at the University of Wisconsin, the new seedlings are more resistant to blight, and they're given away free to Boy Scouts.

What can one person do to protect the earth's resources—even a twelve-year-old? A lot, thousands of boys are discovering as they work to save one of God's loveliest creations.

John

Christian missions needed skilled part-time help. Christians needed a way to put their faith into practice. The two needs came together . . .

WHEN BOB SOLD THE PAINT STORE

As our plane landed near La Paz, Bolivia, a herd of llamas scattered from the runway. Tib, our three children and I pressed to the windows to get our first glimpse of the land where we would be spending the next eight months. What we saw was a flat brown desert stretching away to snow-covered mountain peaks.

Then the door of the plane opened and the comfortable cabin pressure evaporated into the thin air of this highest airport in the world, 13,500 feet above sea level.

My typewriter seemed ten times its weight as I struggled down the airplane steps. Tib followed, sucking in the air in great gulps.

"How in the world," she said between gasps, "do we happen to be here?"

The answer to that question is actually the story of another trip. A year earlier I had stepped off another plane in Jackson, Mississippi. The man I had come to interview for *Guideposts* was there to meet me. In his thirties and balding, Bob Kochtitzky had a Southern accent and a wonderful handshake. A few miles from the airport Bob pointed to a large, prosperous-looking paint store.

"I used to own that store," he said. "But nine years ago I got the most incredible feeling that God was telling me to sell it. He didn't give reasons. Just: *sell the store*. So I did. I put the money in the bank and wondered what would come next."

But months passed and still no further direction came. After almost a year Bob decided to enter seminary, thinking perhaps he was supposed to become a minister. But about the same time another idea came to him. Suppose he were to take some money from the sale of his store and volunteer his paintbrush skills to some overworked missionary. Why, during school vacations he could paint a church, a school, a small hospital somewhere.

"I was so naive," Bob said as we drove along, "that I wrote to my own missions' board offering to pay my own way wherever they needed a short-term volunteer. But there was simply no way for laymen to lend their skills to the missions for short periods of time."

Bob had to bypass his board and apply directly to a missionary he knew of in the Philippines. That summer, 1959, Bob painted the mission school building in Mindanao. In addition he helped deliver supplies to outpost churches, trudging six hours at a stretch through jungle and swamp to isolated mountain communities.

"And when I came back I knew at last why God wanted me to sell that paint store. The greatest benefit from the trip was not to the mission but to me. I knew I had found one way to make religion real to everyday people like myself.

"And here's where I ended up!" Bob waved his arm toward a one-story concrete-block building where he rented a small office. "Not in the pulpit at all."

Bob had, in fact, gone on to seminary, graduated and been ordained a deacon with the rest of his class. But almost at once he had turned in his papers. God's orders were clear at last. He was to work for his vision of service to missions and felt he could do this job best as a layman. In his rather bare headquarters, surrounded by the clatter of machinery in neighboring offices, Bob told how he had campaigned for the chance to set up a pilot program. Already he had the name for the service: *Laos*. The letters were the initials for "Laymen's Overseas Service," but they also spelled the ancient Greek word, *laos*, "the ordinary people of the church."

Where, Bob wondered, should the very first *Laos* volunteer serve? Getting to the Philippines was too expensive, so he looked at South America. During an eight-week visit there in 1962 he drew up a list of ninety-two badly needed jobs which could be handled by volunteers. Six months later the first official *Laos* worker, a construction engineer who had three months between jobs, tackled the first of the South American projects.

This initial experiment was such a success that the next year sixteen volunteers—receiving no salary, paying their own expenses—were sent overseas from *Laos*, and the year after that, forty-eight workers. Bob provided the volunteers with a short, intensive training course covering current problems in the country they'd be visiting, spelling out in flat, almost harsh, terms the difficult facts of modern missionary life.

Far from discouraging volunteers, by 1966 *Laos* had a hundred workers serving in ten countries. They came from all age groups, from college students to retired people. There were Methodists, Presbyterians, Roman Catholics, Baptists. Skills ranged from medicine to potato farming, librarians to maintenance workers. The length of service ranged from a month to several years.

As word of *Laos* spread among understaffed missions both abroad and here at home, Bob began to receive far more requests than he could fill. That was where he hoped a *Guideposts* article might come in: to help him find the volunteers.

"Bob," I said, leaning forward, "you've got five already."

I told him how *Guideposts* had sent our family to Africa for a year to interest young journalists in the possibilities of inspirational writing. "We've been wanting to try the same experiment in South America, but haven't known where to start . . ."

Bob was already at his files. "Writers!" he said. "Wonderful. Now in La Paz, Bolivia . . ."

And that was how we came to be standing at an airport in the Andes. We had already spotted, on the other side of the customs barrier, the man with whom Bob's miraculous files had put us in contact: Paul McCleary, head of the Methodist Church in Bolivia.

"Don't lift those bags!" he called as the inspector finished with them. "You mustn't lift anything till you get used to the altitude." And struggling under the whole load himself he led us out to the mission truck. Soon we were barreling across the treeless plain, that lonely terrain we had first observed from the plane window.

Where was La Paz?

As far as the eye could see in every direction stretched the level, barren land, dotted here and there with tiny adobe huts and rimmed with mountains. And yet a sign at the airport had welcomed us to the country's capital, a city of 200,000 people.

And then suddenly we were peering over the rim of a canyon. Down its sides tumbled a great city, 50,000 tin roofs glinting in the cold mountain sun. We clutched the seats as the truck plunged down the narrow road cut into the cliff face. Instead of a railing, the city had erected a platform bearing the just recognizable remains of a car which had gone too close to the edge.

Below us spread the incredible life and color of La Paz: Indian women in bowler hats sitting beside their heaps of potatoes, the reds and oranges and purples of their shawls taking the place of the flowers and trees of other cities.

We knew from Bob Kochtitzky's no-nonsense study program that the life expectancy of a Bolivian tin miner was thirty years and that half of Bolivia's children die before they are five. In fact we passed several of these pathetic funerals that morning, little groups winding slowly on foot up to the cemetery on the plain above, a tiny white coffin carried on a shoulder.

We had been prepared for poverty and grief in Bolivia.

But we had not been prepared for the beauty. The heart-stopping grandeur of the mountains, the air—or lack of it—so pure and clean that you feel as if a lifelong film has been brushed from your eyes.

"You know," I said to Tib, "I'm kind of glad Bob sold the paint store."

John

There are some needs we hesitate to get involved in . . .

THE SKUNK

It was a rustling in the woods that made me glance out the window beside my word processor. At the edge of the trees I caught sight of a skunk, his black-and-white pattern echoing the dappled light. He seemed to be furiously busy—burrowing maybe? My knowledge of skunks began and ended with that appalling odor.

Next moment, though, the animal emerged from beneath the trees and ran zigzagging across the lawn: plumelike tail, striped back and . . . where his head should have been, a bizarre-looking yellow helmet. As he came closer I saw what the "helmet" was. A six-ounce plastic yogurt container.

The carton struck a rock, and the creature whirled in another direction, only to bump up against our picnic table. For a second he stood still, shaking his head frantically. But the yogurt carton was cone-shaped, the narrow mouth wedged fast about his neck. The skunk charged blindly back into the woods.

I stared after him in dismay. How long since he had forced his head into that carton to reach some bit of food on the bottom? How long had he been running in darkness and terror?

189

It would be the work of a second for me, I thought, to pull that thing off. But the idea of pursuing a skunk through the undergrowth kept me immobilized at the window. How would I ever catch him? And then what? In his panic wouldn't he be certain to spray me?

I sat down and tried to pick up the thread of the story due in the mail that afternoon. But I could think only of an animal running till he dropped from exhaustion. Mustn't this sort of thing have happened before? Might animal experts know what to do?

From the kitchen telephone I dialed the local ASPCA. "We handle domestic animals," the woman told me. "You want the State Conservation Department." She gave me a number in New Paltz, New York.

New Paltz meant a toll call. Anyhow, by now the skunk must be a long way off. Maybe someone else would see him. Someone braver and more athletic.

I dialed the number in New Paltz. A man in the Department of Wildlife listened to my story, then held a muffled conversation. "As long as skunks can't see you," he said into the phone, "they don't spray."

Well . . . that sounded all right, as long as the skunk's head was inside the container. "What happens after the carton comes off?" I asked.

"Just make sure," the man advised, "that he doesn't feel threatened."

I wondered how one went about reassuring a terrified skunk.

"You could throw a blanket over him," Wildlife suggested. "Then run while he's finding his way out."

"That might work," I said, but I must have sounded as unsure as I felt, because the man asked where I was calling from and began looking up names of conservation officers in my area.

How long would it take, I wondered, for someone to get here? Where would the skunk be by then? Standing there in the kitchen, I was gripped by a sudden, strange urgency. I thanked the man, hung up and ran outside. Without stopping to change out of my next-to-best slacks (does skunk scent ever wash out?) and forgetting about the blanket approach, I ran up our driveway to the road.

Of course the skunk wasn't there. Nor did I know why I was. In his frenzy, when I'd seen him last, the animal had been heading the opposite way, straight down the hill into the woods.

But my feet never slowed. I turned left and dashed down the street as though rushing to a long-ordained appointment. I'd run perhaps a hundred yards when a black-and-white streak emerged from the bushes beside the road and ran straight at me, the carton bumping the pavement with each step. I'd stooped down and grabbed hold of the yogurt carton before the astonishment of actually finding the skunk hit me.

The animal was tugging and twisting, unexpectedly strong, to get away. *If they can't see you they won't spray.* His front claws scrabbled against the slippery yellow plastic, his body strained backward, and still he could not wrench free of the carton's viselike neck. It took both of my hands tugging the other way before a small black head suddenly popped free.

And there we stood, facing each other, two feet apart.

I don't know what *he* saw, and how threatening or not the apparition was, but what *I* saw was a sharp quivering nose, two small round ears, and alert black eyes that stared straight into mine.

For fully ten seconds we held each other's gaze. Then the skunk turned, ran a few yards and vanished into the mouth of the culvert that runs beneath the road.

For a moment more I stood there, looking after him. Three minutes could not have passed since I hung up the telephone in the kitchen.

But a timeless parable had played itself out, I thought as I headed back down the drive. The skunk was all those needs I hesitate to get involved in: *Involvement takes time and I have deadlines to meet. I probably can't do anything anyway. Somebody else can handle it better. Besides, involvement can be ugly, and the stench may rub off on me.*

And all these things, of course, may be true. But I've got a yellow pencil holder on my desk, a rather scratched and battered one, to remind me that every now and then God's answer to a need is me.

Elizabeth

It was home to some of the nation's jobless.

THE BRIDGE ON ROUTE 59

We walked beneath Christmas garlands draped from the restaurant ceiling and stepped into the New York night. Snow was falling. The theater where Tib and I were headed was just a few blocks away and we set off filled with the joy of the season. As we rounded a corner, we saw them.

At first I didn't realize that those were people, huddled there on the sidewalk. I thought they were plastic bags, dumped against the side of the building. Then one of the bags moved and I saw that a man and a woman were crouched over a subway ventilation outlet, trying to keep warm in the snow. Beside them were half a dozen soggy paper bags and a suitcase.

"Those are people!" I whispered to Tib as soon as we were out of earshot.

We stole a look back. There was no telltale bottle of cheap wine that so often spells out the individual tragedy of street people. We walked on, the way one does. But in our warm theater seats I kept thinking about our two fellow beings out there in the cold.

When we passed the place on the way to the train

station, hours later, the man and woman were still there and I did one of those foolish things, half apology, half denial, that reveals our deep uneasiness in the face of poverty. As we walked by I reached down into the snow and pretended to be picking up a couple of bills.

"Did you drop these?"

The man took the money quickly and for a brief moment I caught his eye. I'll never forget that look. Nor his words. "I'm not a bum, you know," the man said. "I'm out of work."

It was my first encounter with what had been until that moment only impersonal newspaper statistics on rising unemployment. "The New Poor," the media dubbed them, but now for me—though I never saw this particular couple again—the newly poor had faces and a voice, and a claim on my involvement that grows stronger as the days pass. Since I am a journalist, this involvement started with asking questions. Who are these people? What can we do to help?

The statistics sum it up all too clearly. There was, as of that Christmas season, 1982, a 10.5 percent unemployment rate nationwide. This meant that over eleven million Americans wanted to find work and could not. But even that staggering figure did not reflect the true dimensions of the problem because it left out the underemployed and the discouraged who had simply stopped looking for a job.

What happens to a man or woman whose job is terminated? Unemployment benefits—for those who qualify—help for twenty-six weeks of pounding the pavement. When that's used up, if there's still no work in their area, many people move. They go somewhere else where they believe there *is* work. One by lonely one, families have been making this decision, especially in the states hardest hit by factory shutdowns: West Virginia, Michigan, Ohio, Indiana and Illinois. In their aggregate thousands they head for the Sun Belt, high in hopes and voicing the wisdom of the down-but-not-defeated: "If I have to starve, at least I don't have to freeze."

The only trouble is, there's no work in the Sun Belt either—not for so many . . .

Lester Welshans is thirty-eight years old, a house painter from Mount Pulaski, Illinois. During the seventies things went all right for Les and his wife Sharon and their two kids. The rented house they lived in was roomy, if a little inconvenient, an old farmhouse outside town where rents were low. Sharon had a job too. Although her work as a nurse's aide paid only minimum wage, it helped keep Les junior, born in 1971, and Kimberly Ann, born in 1974, in nice outfits, and it supplied a few extras at Christmastime, such as those expensive Jitterbug lures that young Les and his dad took on fishing trips together.

In 1979 Les noted with alarm that calls for house painting were falling off. By 1980 they had almost ceased. In 1981, none at all. Sitting around all the time, having to make do with Sharon's skimpy wage of $3.35 an hour, Les began to hear stories of how good things were in Texas. "If it takes you fifteen minutes to get a job in Houston, you're doing something wrong," Les heard. Why not give it a try? Besides, he and Sharon had been quarreling lately. Les suspected he was taking some terrible fear out on his wife.

So, along with an estimated million other hopeful men and women, Les decided to leave home in search of something better. He piled a few things into his '71 Ford pickup, kissed his family good-by for a few weeks, and headed south.

In the beginning it looked as if he had made the right decision. In Houston he found a few houses to paint. Not enough, though, to send money home and still pay room rent. So he didn't rent a room: he pulled his truck off the highway at the bridge where the San Jacinto River passes under Highway 59, outside town. Scores of newcomers had made the same decision, and there was a regular community of trucks and vans and tents spread out along the river.

"It's not too bad, for a while at least," Les said to Sharon over the phone. "But I wouldn't want little Les and Kimberly here. The kids living here take an awful ribbing at school. They call them 'Bridge Rats'!"

Soon the recession worked its way into Houston too and house painting jobs fell off. More and more families congregated beneath the 59 bridge and other locations in the Houston area. They weren't welcomed. In some locales, ordinances were passed making tent cities illegal, or making it a misdemeanor to sleep on a park bench. The message was clear: "Keep moving, Stranger!" Vigilante groups in some parts of the Southwest sat outside squatter towns and blew sirens all night to chase the people away. Elsewhere police and dog teams moved in. When would this begin to happen at the 59 bridge?

Les hadn't worked in weeks. He had only a few dollars left, no food, not even gasoline money. Every time he called the Houston job exchange he got the same answer: "No work today. Call back tomorrow." To make matters worse, around Thanksgiving, 1982, word began to go around that 59 bridge people would soon be asked (politely, if possible) to get moving.

But where would they move to? "I was already feeling beat when I called my wife," Les says. "There was no work, and people were calling us bums and drifters. When I told Sharon I might just as well come home to Mount Pulaski, she said don't bother because our rented farmhouse had just been sold and the new owners were coming with a bulldozer to tear it down." Sharon had tried to find another rental, she told Les, but everywhere landlords were asking three months' rent in advance, and on $3.35 an hour you don't save any ahead.

That was Les and Sharon's dark, dark hour.

But, unknown to either of them, help was coming. Weeks earlier one man had seen the need, one pair of hands had been readied. His name was Ray Meyer, a short, blond fellow with glasses who looked like any other out-of-work squatter. Les had noticed him hanging around the 59 bridge.

After that devastating phone conversation with his wife, Les was kicking the tires of his truck when this little blond guy strolled over and asked if he needed anything.

"Need anything! Listen, mister, what I need is some way to bring my wife and kids down here from Illinois. And a place to put them when they get here. And something for them to eat, and a lot of other things I don't have. No money. No job. No prospects. No hope. That's me."

"That's not you," said Ray Meyer. "First thing to do is go get your family! When you come back I'll at least guarantee you a campsite on private land where dogs and sirens aren't going to run you off."

"Who are you?" Les asked.

Ray shrugged. "A street preacher is one of the nicer things I've been called. Does it matter, as long as I can help?"

A little abrasive, sometimes controversial, Ray Meyer had wandered the world as an independent missionary, supporting himself by repairing television sets, ministering chiefly to the needy and the forgotten. He was working among the poor in France when he heard the Lord tell him to go back home to the United States. Ray obeyed, being guided eventually to Houston. Why oil-rich Houston, Ray wondered, when his sympathies were with the down-and-out?

But as he settled in, making a frugal living at his trade, Ray began to realize that not all of Houston was thriving. Every day on his rounds he saw people not just camping but living in cars and trucks. The scenes reminded him of photographs of the Great Depression: the food cooked over outdoor fires, the clothesline strung between trees, the men hanging around at midday. One morning early in 1982 he drove down to the largest of the under-bridge camps and made some friends. It was easy to do; anyone showing interest was welcomed as a novelty.

Soon Ray was visiting wholesale grocery outlets, retail food stores and restaurants, driving his car back to the camps loaded with edible but not saleable foodstuffs. He scrounged for other basics—diapers, soap, gasoline. The Bridge people themselves, new to poverty and shamed by it, would not beg. But Ray Meyer wasn't shy about positioning himself at a stoplight up in town and asking motorists for donations. Many were glad to assist, others were embarrassed at the revelation of poverty in their midst. Some got angry. One truck driver took down a shotgun that he kept in the rear of his cab. "This is what I'd like to give those bums," he told Ray. "And you too."

"You couldn't even nick me," Ray said, his testy side showing, "unless God allowed it. There's a baby girl out on Route 59 who needs to get to a doctor . . ." The truck drove off.

In mid-1982 Ray heard that the squatters were to be evicted from public property. They were a rowdy bunch, the argument went, and anyhow if you gave them food they just sold the stuff for booze. Some of this was true. Ray himself had to stop deliveries to a few of the Bridge folks. But what about the vast majority, the plucky middle-class men and women who were trying so hard to get started again?

Where would they go? A camp on private property would be an answer, but Ray had no money to buy land.

Eventually he talked a landowner into renting him a few acres, cheap. The property was swampy, flooded by the same river that flowed under the 59 bridge. With his own hands Ray started constructing temporary cabins mounted on oil-barrel rafts so they could ride out the frequent floods. It was to this camp, The Shelter, that Ray invited Les Welshans to bring his family.

Within the day Les had found a ride with a man who was heading back to Illinois. It was just before Christmas when he and Sharon, with Les junior, now eleven, and Kimberly Ann, eight—one family like tens of thousands of others across America—set out through the snow in Sharon's 1974 Dodge Coronet. They were not sure the old car could make it, but their hearts were not as heavy as they might have been. They knew somebody was waiting for them in that sprawling Texas town, somebody who had said, "I can help."

In fact, the Welshanses' car didn't make it. On Christmas Eve, 1982, the day after Tib and I attended the theater in New York, Les and Sharon's car broke down. They were twenty miles from Houston and it took their last bit of cash to pay a tow truck to haul them to the 59 bridge.

Kimberly Ann looked up at her father. "Is this where we're going to live, Daddy?"

"Not for long, honey," Les assured her, because walking toward the broken-down Dodge was a short, blond man whose glasses could not conceal the caring in his eyes.

In January, 1983, Les and Sharon moved to The Shelter. Soon afterward Sharon found a job in Houston as a nurse's aide, and Les discovered that he could clear about $10 a day, after paying for gasoline, by picking up beer cans along the highways and selling the aluminum. In his spare time he did volunteer construction work for new arrivals to The Shelter.

Meanwhile Les and Sharon and the kids started working together on a place of their own. Their house is just down the road from The Shelter. It's only one room, and the last time I spoke to Ray Meyer on the phone, it still had no electricity or water, but with a down payment of fifty dollars and an equal amount each month, it's on its way to being the Welshanses' very own.

That's where their Christmas will be celebrated this year, when they get home from the service at Ray's newly consecrated church. There'll be a tree and some new (well, different) clothes for Sharon and Les and some new (really new) things for the kids to wear. And it wouldn't surprise me if Les and Les Junior find a couple of Jitterbugs under the tree with a card from their friend Ray Meyer.

In the six months since Tib and I stepped around a couple huddled in the snow on a sidewalk, we have come to know in a new and visceral way that a plunge from riches to rags can overtake millions of ordinary citizens right here in the United States; forces totally beyond our control can overwhelm us. We also know in a new way that whether the overall economy is labeled "good" or "bad," there will always be pockets of poverty. The encouraging side of our discoveries has been to find a network of caring people spread out across the country. People who see the poor not as "them" but as "us." Followers of Jesus who become His hands stretched out to those in need.

John

What can you and I do about the hungry
and the homeless in our midst?

HOW TO: HELP WHEN PEOPLE HURT

How we respond to hurting people depends in part on the need nearest us—migrant workers? industrial layoffs? abused children? the elderly?—and in part on ourselves. Do we have special skills? Physical limitations? More time than money? Are we starters or joiners?

From hundreds of recent examples, here are four answers which may suggest your own.

■ It takes a certain kind of person to be a starter: the ability to see supply as well as need. For years James Johnson, an artist in Fresno, California, fretted about the tons of edible fruit and vegetables rotting in heaps by the roadside. This was excess production, kept off the market to insure fair prices for the growers.

As jobless and hungry people—the need—began streaming into California, Johnson wondered if he couldn't put the two together. Why not set up a self-help cannery to process all that wasted food! Work would be done by the unemployed themselves as well as by volunteers.

His vision set off a chain reaction of generosity in the San Joaquin Valley. Land for the cannery was given, building materials delivered free of charge. With local labor unions volunteering their skills, and produce donated by local growers, "St. Anthony's Bread Basket" opened in 1983.

■ Sometimes a group of people will catch a vision that singly they might have missed. Rob and Carolyn Johnson, Ed Loring and Murphy Davis were members of a Bible study at a small church in downtown Atlanta, Georgia. From their reading of Scripture it seemed to them that Christ was calling His Church to a more personal involvement with the poor than simply a donation in the plate.

Responding to the call, these four helped make the sanctuary of their church, Clifton Presbyterian, available to the homeless. Fourteen Atlanta churches had soon joined the night shelter program, providing beds each evening for at least a thousand homeless people. An important part of the concept: almost nine hundred more fortunate Atlantans take turns staying alongside those in need.

"I never had a chance to know a poor person before," reported one Atlanta teenager who spent the night with her parents and a hundred destitute men, women and children. "The thing that surprised me is how much like us they are. They are us, only without money."

■ Lest folks like me panic at such stories because they demand so much time, people have come up with simpler ideas too. In the late seventies Blair Hatt, then a student at General Theological Seminary on Ninth Avenue in New York, noticed large numbers of people coming to the front desk looking for a handout. Some were the New Poor, others habitual alcoholics. Hatt and his friends wanted to help, but was it right to give money to addicts who might use it to hurt themselves further? To solve the dilemma, Hatt initiated a program in which General hands out tokens that can be exchanged at a nearby delicatessen: the tokens are not to be honored for alcohol or tobacco.

■ On the other side of the continent there's a small shelter run by an unusual Christian order—different in part because the nuns and monks are allowed to marry.

As the recession of the eighties worsened, the forty-seven brothers and sisters at Raphael House in San Francisco became concerned over families evicted from their homes and forced to place their children in foster care.

Located in a remodeled hospital, Raphael House offers temporary housing and follow-up counseling to families in crisis. If people can't pay the small rent requested, they can stay anyway. What makes this possible? Not only is the entire staff unpaid, but members of the order take jobs in the outside community and contribute their salaries toward expenses. These men and women practice voluntary poverty—they prefer the word "simplicity"—so that others may make a new start. With their lives they demonstrate the meaning of the name Raphael: "God has healed."

Which, it seems to me, is the promise held out to all of us who long to help where people hurt. God will do the healing; our job is only to find our individual assignment in His compassionate plan.

John

PART FIVE

SEEING GOD AS OUR SUPPLY

It's universal, the fear of not
having enough . . .
    enough time,
      enough strength,
       enough money.

To run out of these things,
however, is to discover a
magnificent truth: when we reach
the end of our own resources
God's are just beginning.

A Pfennig for You
The coin wasn't worth much. The message behind it was priceless.

The Caller
He was ten years old when his mother shared her secret.

The Music We Almost Lost
A Jew rescued this Christian music for the church.

The Prayer God Always Answers
It can help us survive in a brusque urban world.

The Competitor
What happens when the competition is in your own home?

The Void I Couldn't Fill
For years she dreamed of a place where she'd feel accepted.

I Like Tax Time!
A song on the radio suggested a new approach.

The Tradition
There are times when we want everything just as it was.

Each week the dollar was worth less.

A PFENNIG FOR YOU

In 1987 while Tib and I were on a sixteen-month free-lance writing stint in Europe, God spoke to me about supply. It was the year of the dollar devaluation. Week after week we watched the money we'd brought with us shrink against other currencies. As our cost of living soared, so did my anxiety.

I was at my most anxious one morning when I pulled into a self-service gas station just off one of the autobahns in Germany. The dollar's latest plunge had brought fuel to the equivalent of three dollars a gallon, and I was muttering to myself as I turned on the pump and watched the "amount due" dial spin faster than my eye could follow.

At that moment I noticed a young man ambling up the street in my direction. Wearing stained corduroy trousers and a torn sweater, he had the childlike look that so often goes with mental retardation. He stopped and stood watching me fill the tank.

As I withdrew the nozzle the young man edged closer and at first I thought he wanted a ride. But he had drawn a small purse from his pocket and was fumbling with the clasp. He emptied a few coins into his hand and with clumsy fingers selected one of them.

"Fur dich," he said. *For you.* He held out a one-pfennig piece, worth less than half a U.S. cent.

"For me? But I don't need . . ."

I stopped short. In fact I had just been feeling very much in need. I stood there with the gasoline hose in one hand, the little copper in the other, watching God's spokesman wander off up the street.

"For you . . ." These are the words He speaks to each of us out of His infinite supply. *There is enough for you.*

John

When you're tired out and the job's not done, where does the strength come from? A railroad worker discovers God's supply.

THE CALLER

John Mealing tells his story to John

I remember that summer afternoon in 1925, because that was the day Mama told me how she kept going when she was all tuckered out.

On that hot afternoon, Mama and I and my seven brothers and sisters had just come in from the fields where we'd been picking beans in the scorching Alabama sun. We were tired right to the bone and we all flopped down—everyone except Mama. She went to the sink and started to wash her face because she had to go out again. Mama was raising us by herself and that took two jobs: she worked in the fields, then evenings she went to cook dinner for the family of a section foreman on the railroad.

I'd often wondered how she found her strength. The answer, I knew, had to lie somehow in her singing. Mama would sing in church, of course, but she'd sing with just as much heart in the fields or over the washtub—like she was pulling energy from her songs. And that summer afternoon, when I was just a little boy of ten and very tired, she put her secret into words.

"John, when you're down, that's the time to sing," Mama told me as she headed out the door for the foreman's house. "Sing until the Power comes."

That was all she said, but it was enough—though I had no idea then how large Mama's words were going to be in my life.

I used to dream I could quit picking beans and chopping cotton and get me a railroad job on the Western Alabama. When I was eleven my chance came. The foreman told Mama he needed a water boy; I could have the job if I was strong enough to handle it.

My very first day I learned what he meant about being strong. The farmer's pond where I had to go for water was five miles from where the gang was working. It was easy going to the pond, but coming back up the line, with the bucket sloshing against my knee, that was hard. The men always dipped more water than they needed. They took one good drink from the ladle and poured the rest on the ground. If ever I got me a man's job on the work gang, I wouldn't treat the water boy like that.

I kept asking the Lord if He'd please get me a regular job lining rail. I really admired the men in our section. I'd watch a dozen of them lift a rail that weighed just under a ton, walk it forward and join it just where the foreman wanted. They could move rail like that all day because they worked to singing. One man from the gang kept the beat, slow and easy, with a little chant. He was known as a "caller."

"Move it, boys, can you move it?"

"Ye—ah!" the men would call back, and everybody'd lift at once and that piece of rail would move!

I was nearly in my teens by that time—and big too—and I knew I could handle a man's work if I got the chance. But when another year passed and I was still toting water, I said to myself the time had come to get the foreman's attention.

Over the months I'd made friends with the engineer of a local train that steamed by our section, and on an unusually hot day I asked him to give me a block of ice from off his refrigerator car.

That noon the men got ice in their water. Now, if you're working in Alabama when the summer corn is high, you don't drink ice water unless you plan to sit down or fall down. The men drank that ice water, but then they weren't about to go on working. When the foreman saw his crew lolling about and found out what'd happened, he said, "You want to get fired, John?"

"No, sir," I answered him. "I just want to get fired off this job. Seems like I'm not very good at it." The foreman laughed—and let me join the section gang.

Then came the big flood in 1928 that gave me a dream.

That high water caused a washout down below Montgomery. Tracks and telegraph poles were jackstrawed into the red-earth cornfields. Even before the water went down, the railroad had us working in shifts, day and night, trying to get the trains running again. We were so tired out we began to make mistakes, like dropping rail; one of us could have got hurt real bad. I once saw a man die in shock when a rail dropped and bounced and shattered both his legs.

One morning following the flood we woke to a commotion. An extra gang had come down from Atlanta, a team of forty men who were specialists. Our section gang may have been good, but these new men were big league. They were the line's troubleshooters, coming in to show us how to build up banks and lay track in a hurry. With the new men we worked all day and on into the night, just like we'd done before, but now there was a difference. Now we could keep going past the end of our strength because of one man—Billy Joe.

Billie Joe was a caller. I'd heard work chants before, as I say, but never from someone so good. Billie Joe could use his voice! He put his whole self into his songs, and you could feel the uplift. With him singing we forgot how tired we were.

> *Oh, come on, boys, let's go around the wall.*
> *Don't want to stumble*
> *and don't want to fall.*
> *That suits me!*
> *Come on, move it. Hey, boys, can you move it?*

The more I listened that morning, the more I knew I had run into someone with the same secret my mother knew. Billie Joe's songs gave you strength! Under him we could lift more loads, work longer hours. Time passed quicker, too, as he sang songs with a story, telling about hard work or women or doing a job right.

Soon as a break came I slipped into the piney woods, hoping I could remember the songs. The tunes were all there, in my head! I didn't like Billie Joe's cuss words, so I left those out and made up my own words to fit the beat.

Oh, my cap'n can't read,
My cap'n can't write.
Cap'n can't tell
When the track is right.
Can you move it? Yeah, can you move it?

I had the knack! Someday when I was older I'd be a caller too.

My chance didn't come for a long time, because the Depression hit and they laid off the newest men. But in 1940, when I was thirty-two, I was hired back on the railroad.

One very hot afternoon the job was going slow. We were working hard but we couldn't make that rail *move*. That day I just started to sing, calling alongside the men as we worked.

Now, the foreman there in the Birmingham yards, old man Barfield, he heard me. That day he told me to back off from the rail and keep time for the men with a song.

Way down yonder
on Durand Bend
heard my hammer
whistlin' the wind.
Boys, can you move it? Say, can you move it?

When old man Barfield saw how that whole track got to jumping, I had me a new job.

Well, I worked for the railroads on and off for fifty-one years, mostly as a caller. But then times changed. The need for calling went out as lines began to lay track with machines instead of men. Today, as far as I know, I am the last of a kind.

Too bad, because something beautiful is fading away. I remember days in the Birmingham yards when so many people crowded around as we sang and worked that we had to ask them please to move back.

People came to hear us singing, but it was more than that.

I think they caught something important in the way we worked, watching how everybody pulled together, and noticing how we wouldn't be hurried. We learned the hard way not to be hurried. There was a man once thought I wasn't calling fast enough. He took over the singing, picking up a quicker beat. But that wasn't right. A rail dropped and one of the workmen got his leg broke. You got to have patience if you want to do things the Lord's way.

I'm nearly eighty years old now. The other day I was on my front porch, enjoying the springtime sun, when off in the distance I heard a diesel horn blow. Wasn't a steam whistle like I remember from my young years, but it made me think of the days when I called for the men and it gave them energy.

It's just like Mama said that summer day seventy years ago. You may be down, but there's something you can do.

You can sing until the Power comes. Then the song will carry the load.

> *I got my learnin'*
> *on Number Four*
> *An' now I'm ready to go.*
> *Boys, I'm tellin you . . .*
> *I'm ready to go.*

A grillwork door. A penniless hunchback.
A Jewish grandmother. When God sets the goal,
He also supplies the means . . .

THE MUSIC WE
ALMOST LOST

He was perhaps the greatest musician who ever lived. And the most influential: Western music today is rooted in the work of Johann Sebastian Bach.

And yet, astonishingly, for three generations after his death in 1750, this seminal figure was almost forgotten. Even in his lifetime his music was dismissed as dry and old-fashioned, out of step with the graceful compositions of his own sons. That Bach today has resumed his rightful place is the achievement of another musical genius, Felix Mendelssohn. And the story covers precisely those three generations when Bach's music had passed into oblivion . . .

Seven years before Bach's death, a ragged fourteen-year-old hunchback hobbled up to one of the gates of Berlin and was ordered to apply instead at another gate, the only one through which Jews were permitted to pass. The boy obeyed the sentry's gestures, not his words—Jews were forbidden to learn the German language. He limped on around the wall on feet already blistered by the

eighty-mile trek from his little hometown of Dessau. Re-
buffs and pain did not daunt this youngster, because in
his heart God had planted a goal. The city log at the
"Jews' gate" recorded:

> Today there passed through
> the Rosenthaler Gate: 6 oxen,
> 7 swine, 1 Jew.

The name of the Jew was Moses. He had no family
name—Jews were not allowed them. Many Jewish boys in
that harsh time, however, were named for Israel's great
liberator, and various ways were found to distinguish
them. This Moses was the son of a poor Dessau peddler
named Mendel, and in the Jewish community he was
known as Moses, Mendel's Sohn.

In Berlin's Jewish Quarter Moses found an attic corner
to live in and a few menial chores that permitted him to
purchase a loaf of bread each week. This he marked with
his pencil into six equal parts; on the Sabbath he did not
eat.

On this ration of bread, with water, Moses pursued his
goal for six years. His goal was knowledge, and in Berlin
there were books. Learning to read them was itself an
obstacle that would have stopped a less determined person. "Gentile" languages were forbidden to Moses, not
only by Prussian law but also by the Jewish community.
Over the centuries Jews had made a virtue of the segrega-
tion forced upon them. A Jew so much as caught in
possession of a book in any language other than Yiddish

or Hebrew could be expelled by his own people from the only society to which he could belong.

But when God provides a goal, He also supplies the readiness to sacrifice for it. The hunchbacked lad pursued knowledge as an outlaw, studying at night in his attic corner, hiding books smuggled from no-one-knows-where in the straw of his bed, damaging his eyes in the light of a tallow candle. All alone he taught himself German, French, English, Latin and Greek—and the mathematics, philosophy and literature they opened to him.

Whether he ever heard of Bach, who died at the age of sixty-five when Moses was twenty-one, is doubtful. But the two would have understood each other well. Both had an all-enabling purpose: to honor God. Bach through music, Moses through understanding.

Bach, too, as a boy, had permanently impaired his eyesight in forbidden study. The orphaned Johann Sebastian lived with a much older brother, also a musician, who gave him music lessons with standard student pieces. Possibly out of jealousy for the infinitely greater talents of his young brother, the older Bach kept his collection of more challenging works under lock and key.

The cabinet in which this treasure was shut away, however, had a grillwork front. With his small hands, Johann Sebastian was able to roll the music up and draw it out. Night after night for six months, working by moonlight after the household was asleep, the boy copied these pieces—until his brother discovered him and took away not only the originals but the copies the boy had gained at the expense of his eyes.

Leaving his brother's home at fifteen, Johann Sebastian earned composition lessons by singing in church choirs, sometimes walking as far as a hundred miles for the chance to hear a fine musician perform.

The specifics were different in Moses' case, but the determination was the same. At twenty-one he was hired as a tutor for the children of a Jewish silk merchant. Later he became the accountant for this firm, and still later a partner. Most of his time, however, Moses devoted to writing, book after book, arguing for the emancipation of his people: from persecution without and narrowness within. Known as "the German Socrates," Moses lived to see his books translated into more than thirty languages.

And change the world he lived in. In his personal life, too, the seemingly impossible had happened. Small, deformed, ugly, Moses had married a woman who fell in love with him, sight unseen, through the beauty of his writing. They had a long and happy marriage—and to Moses' children passed his remarkable mind.

It passed especially to one member of this second generation—Moses' son Abraham. Abraham saw earlier than almost anyone else that the just-dawning Industrial Revolution would require a new kind of economics. Which is how the third generation, including Abraham's son Felix, was born to considerable wealth.

Not, however, to ease. The family, now legally surnamed Mendelssohn, remained as motivated and self-disciplined as ever. Only on Sunday were Felix and the other children permitted to sleep late—that is, until six. Other mornings they were awakened at five to practice penmanship or piano scales or irregular Greek verbs. Because it was also a home filled with love, the children thrived on these parental demands. All were bright—Felix a musical prodigy. To give him piano lessons, Abraham engaged the head of Berlin's Singing Academy, Karl Friedrich Zelter.

Zelter was a musical scholar who not only knew of the all-but-forgotten Johann Sebastian Bach, but taught Bach's music to his pupils. Bach's keyboard pieces, that is. Bach's great choral and orchestral masterpieces had not been heard for three generations.

Nor could they be heard.

Choirs no longer sang polyphony, orchestras were ignorant of counterpoint. Indeed, the handful of musical antiquarians who had seen one of Bach's handwritten scores agreed that they were no longer playable.

They reckoned without the grandson of Moses, Mendel's son. The Bach piano pieces Zelter taught Felix became the eight-year-old's passion. When he learned that Zelter himself possessed a manuscript of a vast Bach work called the *St. Matthew Passion,* he pleaded to be allowed to look at it. Why Zelter refused remains a mystery. Possibly he felt that the music was too exalted to be handled by a child, no matter how gifted.

It was young Bach and his older brother's music collection all over again. Felix did not have a grillwork door to help him, but he did have a grandmother. Whether this devout Jewish woman realized that the music her grandson pined for was set to a New Testament text designed to be sung in churches at Easter, no one knows. In any event, to obtain it for Felix she unleashed all the force of her considerable personality.

When Zelter refused to entrust his museum piece into her hands, she tracked down other collectors, and at last uncovered another yellowing manuscript of the *St. Matthew Passion*. Next she hired a skilled copyist to reproduce, note by note, the entire three-and-a-half hours of music.

Felix was fourteen when his grandmother presented him with the massive score. For five years he carried that music about with him, reading a section before going to bed, humming another over his breakfast chocolate. He lived it, he absorbed it into himself.

He became, meanwhile, an international celebrity owing to the brilliance of his own music. But, like his grandfather Moses, he couldn't let go of the goal he'd set himself at age fourteen. Somehow Bach's choral music must be reborn in a live performance. The barriers must have seemed every bit as forbidding as the city walls of Berlin had to his grandfather so many years before. Zelter, Bach devotee though he was, dismissed out of hand the idea that the singers in his academy—the best Berlin had to offer—could master such archaic music. The other adults that Felix appealed to were equally discouraging.

He was eighteen when he gained his first ally, a twenty-six-year-old actor and singer named Eduard Devrient. Felix played for him some of the music for the words of

Jesus—and won him on the spot. It took Felix and Eduard another year, but at last, worn down by their combined efforts, Zelter gave in and granted the two young men permission to recruit from his Singakademie the one hundred and fifty-eight singers required for the chorus, and to use the large academy hall for the performance—though he warned that without some lighter, more modern music on the program they would not fill a tenth of it.

Now Felix approached the leading singers of the city to take the solo parts. He engaged top musicians—Abraham supplying the money—for the enormous orchestra, coached each ensemble component himself. In a day when one full-scale rehearsal was considered thorough preparation, Felix conducted nine.

And gradually word spread through Berlin that something out of the ordinary was taking place at the Singakademie. The day the tickets went on sale every last one was snatched up in the first hour, with more than one thousand music-loving Berliners turned away.

Felix was a shock to the distinguished audience, including the Prussian king and his court, when he stepped onto the podium on the evening of March 11, 1829. Accustomed to conductors with broad stomachs and silver beards, they saw a slender young man one month out of his teens who carried not a scrap of music with him. Felix knew every note of the vast creation by heart—had held it in his heart from the age of fourteen.

From the opening bars a church-like hush fell over the hall. The chorus sang, the orchestra played as though it were the only night of music they would ever make. In a day of flamboyant conducting styles, Felix used as few and as simple gestures as possible, signaling his musicians with a glance or a nod, his face shining with the glory of what he was hearing. In the audience men and women alike were weeping, including those in the lobby and hallways, where doors were left open so that the overflow crowd could hear.

"Isn't it strange," said Felix to Eduard, who had sung the role of Jesus, when the tumultuous ovation at the close of the long evening slacked off at last, "that an actor and a Jew should have to give back to the world its greatest Christian music?"

There had to be a repeat performance ten days later, a third on Good Friday. Already word about the long-neglected composer was racing across Europe. Bach's other religious masterworks were being dug out of church storerooms; publishers who a month earlier would have laughed at the very idea of offering such works to the public were rushing to be the first to get them into print.

Johann . . . Moses . . . Felix. Strange that a Jew should restore Bach's sacred music to the church? Not when we know who plants "impossible" goals in the hearts of the young.

Elizabeth

Is it possible to live gently in a jarring world?

THE PRAYER GOD
ALWAYS ANSWERS

I was wheeling an empty shopping cart up the aisle of the supermarket when an angry shout stopped me.

"Hey! Bring that thing back here!"

I released the cart with apologies—but it was not so easy to let go of the backlash in my emotions.

In a crowded world unpleasant brushes with strangers are inevitable. The question is not whether we will encounter angry people, but how we will deal with the residue of feelings they leave behind.

For years I would let an episode like the one in the supermarket spoil a day. A verbal blast which the speaker doubtless forgot in minutes would ring in my ears for hours.

I'd try every way I knew to erase it from my mind. I'd tell myself I was hypersensitive. I'd picture extenuating circumstances in the individual's life. I'd remind myself how often I too was short-tempered.

And all of this helped. But it left me, if no longer seething, not really free of the experience either.

It was a chance remark by my daughter-in-law that showed me a better way. Meg had enrolled at Tennessee

State University in Nashville. "People are so helpful," she commented when she phoned to report on her first week of classes. She went on to describe a friendly registrar, an accommodating librarian.

People are so helpful . . . Didn't I find that true of most strangers too? Considerate, courteous, kind. The problem with the way I'd been handling the occasional abrasive individual was that it kept my attention fixed on that negative encounter.

What if, the next time I met one of these upset and upsetting folks, I asked God to bring across my path that day an exceptionally pleasant person? Suppose, in fact, I asked Him to bring me *three* such people?

I had a chance to try it a few days later when a parking attendant bellowed that the lot I was trying to enter was full. His foul language was still reverberating in my ears as I backed into a space at the curb. "Please, Lord, show me three people who . . ."

I hadn't even finished the prayer before I saw him in the rearview mirror: a passerby on the sidewalk, guiding me into the space with hand signals.

At the entrance to the Medical Arts Building around the corner, a teenage boy caught up with me: "You dropped your glove, lady."

And in the optometrist's waiting room on the fifth floor the receptionist paused on her way out. She was going for coffee; could she bring me some, too?

His envoys don't always appear, as they did that first time, within fifteen minutes. But in the years since Meg's phone call, this particular prayer has been answered every single time, without exception. Sales people, post office clerks, bus drivers, one and all exhibiting the graciousness of human nature.

Perhaps the prayer opens my eyes to the friendliness that's there all along. Perhaps God works a homely miracle, time after time. I only know that the inevitable bruisings of urban life no longer cast a pall over the day. Oh, I seethe for a moment, sure. But it's only a moment. As fast as I can I release the offending party from my judgment.

And then? Then I wait eagerly to meet the three delightful strangers God will bring my way today.

Elizabeth

Suppose what God gives you isn't as good as
what He gives someone else?

THE COMPETITOR

The other day a banker friend asked me to play a game which was going the rounds at her office. She showed me a check designed for a joint account, with the names of both husband and wife printed at the top. "See anything unusual?" she asked.

"Sure," I said. "The wife's name is over the husband's."

My friend laughed. "Now I know something about you," she said. "People who answer that fast have a lot of competition in their marriage."

Later, thinking over that little Rorschach test, I realized that my friend was right. I've been competitive with Tib since the day we were married. I also realized that this no longer bothers me: years ago Tib and I faced the issue of competitiveness in marriage and have learned something about how to handle it.

The problem itself was a rarity only a few years ago. After the Civil War my grandparents left their ruined home in South Carolina and migrated to Texas. They took with them touches of the Old South, including the fact that Grandmother called Grandfather "Mr. Sherrill." It was symbolic of the comfortable distance that existed between them. In their new home Grandmother ran the house, tended the garden beneath the creaking windmill and looked after five children while Mr. Sherrill struggled until late at night to keep the hardware store alive, down on the square.

Our children, on the other hand, started married life with a very different set of unspoken rules. For them the boundary between marriage roles is less distinct. Our son Donn and his wife, Lorraine, for example, both have graduate degrees in business administration, both took opening jobs at approximately the same salary, both cook a mean veal parmigiana.

The potential for competition between Donn and Lorrie—and between millions of other husbands and wives in the 1990s—is easy to detect. Is this good or bad, or simply different? In America we're accustomed to hailing competition as a beneficial thing, improving performance all around, responsible for most of the gains of our history. But in marriage? Isn't marriage supposed to be the very model of cooperation? What happens when competition crops up in this traditional haven of support?

I will never forget the bewilderment I felt on the day it first dawned on me that I was in competition with the girl I also loved and wanted to see succeed. Because of my five years in the army, Tib and I found ourselves at the close of World War II starting our junior year of college together. It felt good to be back in school where I'd been accustomed to placing at the top of my class. Only . . . now in every course there was this student who got better grades than I did.

My wife.

The Swiss university we were attending followed the European custom of posting test results in a public place, in order of ranking. The first, the second time Tib scored higher than I, I was hearty in my congratulations. On the morning that Tib's name was posted in first place for the third time in a row, a fellow student said to me, "Doesn't it make you proud, having your wife always number one?" Again, I was hearty in my agreement. A little too hearty, perhaps?

I don't think it was a conscious decision—or not very conscious—to see to it that I enrolled in different classes from Tib's from then on. During the post-college years we built a very positive marriage. We created a family together, stood together through deaths and cancer, became Christians together. Our cooperation even extended into our careers as we became a writing team.

But competition ignored is not competition eliminated. Curious events kept occurring. One time I wrote to an editor suggesting a two-part article, half to be written from my viewpoint, half from Tib's. The idea was accepted, the double article written and sent off. We were on Nantucket Island at the time the long-awaited answer appeared in our box at the post office. I ripped open the letter which would tell whether or not our son Scott could have the better-quality guitar his instructor recommended.

Yes . . . there was a check inside! But as I scanned the

covering letter my heart began to pound. For, with ridiculous explanations about "balance in the issue," the editor had accepted Tib's article and not mine.

I dashed out of the post office, got in the car and headed up the cobblestoned main street. All the while I was phrasing an answer to this so-called editor, telling him that he could take both articles or neither one.

Fortunately, before I had a chance to get my irate letter into the mail, I was stopped by one of those fragile episodes which are so often the way God speaks to us.

In the shallow water of the Sound in front of our house, that afternoon, I saw a herring gull catch an eel. As the bird headed for shore with his wriggling prey in his beak, another gull swept in on the wind. Rather than let the newcomer snatch even a mouthful of his prize, the first gull dropped the eel and wheeled to attack the marauder. The last I saw of them, the two gulls were in a screaming chase around the sail of a boat while supper swam away.

The parallel was so obvious that I laughed out loud. Was I going to throw away that important check out of sheer animal competitiveness?

Of course not. But equally clear was the fact that competitiveness threatened the harmony of our home. Ignoring the problem had not altered the strength of my emotions. We'd have to try another approach.

So we set out to reduce the potential for competition with an agreement: no more separate writing projects. Henceforth, everything we did would appear under our joint byline. "John and Elizabeth Sherrill" would become a single entity, indistinguishable as individuals.

The device removed competition all right, but a year we spent in England in the 1970s showed us at what cost. England has always been one of our favorite countries—but that year a curious listlessness had settled over the land. We noticed it especially in the shops where government decree made it illegal for a storekeeper to stay open one moment longer than a competitor. And heaven help a gas station owner who carried fishing tackle, even if his business was located on the bank of a river.

Competition, it seemed, was a necessary ingredient for the healthy functioning of living beings. It compels one tree to crowd out another on the forest floor and drives one rutting ram to crash into a competing male with a collision that can be heard for miles. The stronger tree gets the sun, the stronger ram gets his lady, the next generation gets the benefit.

But trees and rams are not social beings; humans *are*. Cooperation is even more essential to our survival than competition. And in that most basic of social units, the partnership between a man and a woman, cooperation is all-important. What then are we to do with this other built-in facet of our make-up, the competitiveness which we can neither ignore nor legislate out of our lives?

One day for a magazine piece—not incidentally under her own byline—Tib interviewed a swimming coach who works with handicapped children. "I know that I'm getting somewhere," he told her, "on the day a youngster stops comparing himself with somebody else."

A normal child could swim to the end of the pool and back in the time it took a handicapped child just to get down the steps. Equal concentration and effort were required in both instances. "The trick," the coach said, "is to get my kids to take their eyes off the next guy. Instead, each youngster has to learn to compete with the best in himself. I tell him he belongs to the Special Order of Competitors."

Even as Tib related the conversation to me, I knew that the coach's insight had application beyond the poolside. It was wisdom for all of us who are scrappers by nature but find ourselves in a situation, such as marriage, where outdoing the other guy is not appropriate. We are probably never going to eliminate our competitive streak. But we can *transform* it.

The interview with the swim coach took place ten years ago. I'm still a competitive person, but I'm learning to redirect that energy so that it becomes a force for improving my own performance, rather than begrudging someone else's.

Today when Tib keeps jogging long after I've run out of breath, I cheer her on—and remind myself that yesterday I slowed down two driveways ago. When her recollection of an event differs from mine—and she turns out to be right—I'm able (after just a minute) to be aware that her attention to detail has improved my own over the years. God's supply to each of us is infinite in grandeur, endless in potential. But we'll never grasp this while we're eyeing someone else's provision instead of our own.

In writing about the swim coach Tib came upon a Bible quote that sums up the changed perspective which has helped me so much.

"Each one," wrote St. Paul to the Galatians, "should test his own actions. Then he can take pride in himself, without comparing himself to somebody else" (Galatians 6:4, NIV).

It's a watchword for all of us who belong to the General Order of Competitors.

John

An actress describes what it was like to grow up without a sense of belonging . . .

THE VOID I COULDN'T FILL

Joan Fontaine tells her story to Elizabeth

For years I used to dream about a place—a place where I would feel deeply at ease, accepted, part of a family. A place where I belonged. By the time I reached my fifties I'd decided no such place existed. Then, in 1972, I found it.

I'm sure the sense of being an outsider started in infancy with ill health and the isolation that went with it. My mother told me that I spent the first two-and-a-half years of my life wrapped from head to toe in cotton bandages due to the eczema that covered me. My father, Walter de Havilland, was a professor teaching at the Imperial University in Tokyo, where I was born. Mother always believed that the goat's milk that is given to babies in Japan started me on my endless succession of ailments.

My parents' marriage was not a happy one. Before I was three, Mother, my sister and I left Japan and settled in Saratoga, California, where doctors assured Mother that the climate would be healthier. It was true that my eczema got better, but just about every other conceivable illness followed. My earliest memories are of tastes—castor oil and Scott's Emulsion and the hatefulness of unsweetened licorice cough syrup—and of white-uniformed strangers bending over me with long, hurting needles.

I suppose it was no wonder that with such handicaps I found it hard to relate to other children. Everything about my life seemed different from theirs. By now my mother had remarried. My stepfather was an investment counselor, but I'm sure he should have been a drill sergeant. The bedroom my sister and I shared, when I wasn't quarantined with some infection, was modeled after a barracks: khaki spreads on iron bedsteads, khaki-painted furniture against dun-colored walls, military-style inspections morning and night. At his insistence, each Sunday we wrote out the schedule for the week ahead:

    7:00—7:15 bathe and dress
    7:15—7:45 breakfast
    7:45—8:15 make beds;
    8:15—8:30 walk to school

and so on through the long, regimented day. My stepfather was a well-intentioned man and I respected him, but he was unable to give the warmth, the open affection, the understanding that I yearned for.

And yet illness and isolation had their compensations, for instead of real companions, I found my friends in books and in the dramatic sketches Mother taught my sister and me to act in when friends came to visit. On days when I was unable to sit up in bed, I would weave long thrilling dramas in my head. Little did I think, at such lonely moments, that I was going through the perfect apprenticeship for an acting career.

But apparently it showed to those around me. One day a friend of Mother's who had seen our little living-room dramas received a call from the actress May Robson. May was looking for a young girl to play the role of the ingenue in her next play.

"Joan de Havilland," said Mother's friend without hesitation. And so I found myself in the wonderful make-believe world of theater.

By now my sister, Olivia de Havilland, was an established actress; in order not to trade on her name I took our stepfather's name, Fontaine. Acting was a strenuous career for a girl as sickly as I was, but I soon came to know why Dame Sybil Thorndike called it "Doctor Theater." No matter how bad I felt or how high my temperature, when the curtains parted, a burst of energy always flooded into me, and I went on, oblivious to everything but the part I was playing.

An increasingly successful movie career had many rewards, but it did not bring me the close relationships that I kept seeking, sometimes desperately. Perhaps it was the longing for a warm father figure that made my expectations of marriage so ridiculously high. My husband was to be everything I had missed as a girl. All-loving, all-strong, all-wise, he would be the answer to every need. And each time an individual man fell short of those expectations the disillusionment was keener, the depression that followed more serious. Each time I felt as if I were a wanderer with no place to go, no place to belong.

It was during one of those bleak times in 1972 that I finally realized what I had been doing. I had been fantasizing a perfect human being, trying to make of the person nearest me what flesh and blood can never be. Even if a man could be the father I dreamed of, the brother I never had, he could never be God. Of course I wanted a solid center to my life, of course I wanted perfect faithfulness, perfect love—it's just that I had been looking for those things in the wrong places.

I remember so well the day, sitting alone in my New York apartment, when that realization came to me. I remember because with it, quietly but clearly, came the answer I had been seeking for so long. Not far away was a tranquil place of worship called the Church of the Heavenly Rest. I began to attend services there. A few months later I consulted the rector, Burton Thomas, and told him I wanted to be baptized. With just a few friends to stand with me, and Dr. Thomas's wife Hazel as my godmother, I entered at last into the place where I belonged.

Baptism is a sign of God's grace—and grace changes people. Have I been changed? I believe so. Where I was judgmental and demanding, I now feel more sympathy for other people. My friends, who seem closer and dearer, tell me that I seem closer and dearer to them. I feel stronger in myself; I'm no longer looking to human beings to supply what only God can give.

Sometimes when a bird sings in Central Park and no one else stops to listen, I feel myself overwhelmed with wonder and gratitude to the Giver. And sometimes I wonder why it took me so long to recognize Him. Then I think of Jesus' parable of the workers in the vineyard, and remember that in God's sight there is no soon or late. In that story each worker received a coin no matter how recently he'd arrived. For me the coin without price is the knowledge that I belong.

How God turned a dreaded chore into a plus.

I LIKE TAX TIME!

Tax time was approaching. Like millions of others, Tib and I would soon be slogging through stacks of bills and canceled checks, attempting to itemize deductions. For years I'd dreaded this chore, putting it off till the last possible moment, grousing about the cost in time and money.

That winter morning I was contemplating the annual ordeal when over the radio came the strains of "Turn, Turn, Turn"—a popular song of the moment based on the passage in Ecclesiastes proclaiming that there is a God-given time for everything we do (Ecclesiastes 3:1).

Everything? Even filling out tax forms?

Well, why not? God knew I had to do my rendering-unto-Caesar. Suppose He'd provided a "right" time for this chore and I was able to recognize it—would it turn the task into something other than sheer drudgery?

I set out to discover this hypothetical moment.

First I actually looked at the calendar, really looked at it, instead of finding to my amazement that April 15 was next week. Then I did a bit of simple subtraction, backing up from the IRS deadline. April 15, minus a cushion week to allow for unexpected interruptions, minus two more weeks for the actual work. This put me at March 25.

Now I subtracted an additional three weeks for "waiting expectantly" for this mysterious right moment . . . whatever in the world that might turn out to be. Which is how I came to March 1 as a reasonable date for starting my experiment.

Cooperation from Tib was important: she had to agree to my keeping papers spread out on a card table in the living room during the wait. Tib watched as I made two cardboard signs with a magic marker: "Income" and "Expenses." On the Income side of the table went the W-2s from our employers, statements from the bank, notice of a bond that had matured. On the other side I put various receipts for deductions.

So far, it was the same procedure as in previous years, except that I'd started early and that this time, as I brought out the different records, I made no effort to organize them. I just spread them out and waited.

And waited.

Several times a day I passed that card table, eyeing the bits of paper like a jigsaw puzzle fan looking for a fit.

Nothing happened. I had been half expecting some sort of this-is-the-moment revelation, but none came. I'd have to slug out my tax return as always.

Then on March 17, more than two weeks after I first spread out my tax papers, it snowed. The plows are always late getting to our street so I had to cancel a lunch date. I lit a fire in the fireplace intending to catch up on some correspondence. As I passed the card table my eyes fell on the date of a canceled check. Casually I began to shuffle a few receipts, putting them in order by month and day as, of course, I'd always done.

This time, though, there was a difference. Always before, I'd been under such last minute pressure to meet the deadline that I only thought about the numbers, never about what the numbers represented.

But . . . these receipts were telling a story! There was the charge-card carbon for a dinner when Tib and I were on a story assignment in Louisiana. "Honey," I called out, "remember that restaurant in New Orleans where we had the crayfish?" For a few moments we relived the trip. A little later I called again, "Do you remember the day when . . ." By the time the fire had died out I'd gone through most of the receipts. And Tib and I had spent a morning reminiscing.

It would be an exaggeration to say that I have looked forward to tax time since that beginning, years ago. But I do find advantages to the process that I never dreamed of when I "made" time for doing my taxes rather than accepting God's moment. Year after year His moment has provided a little time-island in which to step back, review the year, get perspective on our lives.

For one thing, each March we find ourselves appreciative of having an income at all. Our son Donn's business takes him to Latin America where each month he sees people living in cardboard lean-tos on the city dumps: estimating taxes wouldn't seem much of a hardship there.

For another, tax time is an opportunity to look at

giving. The way we spend our money says a lot about what we find important. Some donations are standard, year after year: our church, Oxfam, United Way, ecological concerns. Others are responses to emergency needs: famine, earthquake. Do we have our priorities where they belong?

Little scraps of paper, tax receipts, become snapshots of our lives. Each year has its highlights. Since we work at home, repairs and maintenance are in part deductible, giving us a chance to think about people like the man who came with his teenage son to paint our house. Robert teaches art in our local community college but his real subject is quality. "Will you ever forget Robert and his boy up on those ladders with *vacuum cleaners!*" They'd been sucking away the dust from sanding, to ensure a good bond for the new layer of paint.

And finally, at tax time, we have a chance to think about our nation. We don't agree with everything our taxes go for—who does? But in this land where we tax ourselves, we make the decisions about how our country's money is spent, and that is worth remembering.

Any good planning can keep tax time from being a crisis, but it won't keep it from being a bore. For me the right moment—God's moment—for doing taxes has come to mean expecting a gift from Him, a set-aside time for reviewing the past and making plans for the future. When we find God's timing we can do the first with gratitude, the second with new perspective.

John

In a world of rapid change, can God supply anything as meaningful as what we've lost?

THE TRADITION

"Christmas is the time when nothing ought to change."

Our newly married daughter Liz put into words what all of us were feeling. We had come from our home in New York State to spend the holidays with her and her husband, Alan (ninth-generation Massachusetts), in their new apartment in Tucson, Arizona. Outside, on this day before Christmas, cactus-wrens hopped about the mesquite bushes beneath the blazing desert sun, while indoors the four of us gulped iced tea and longed for pine woods and falling snowflakes.

"Home in Leicester," Alan recalled, "we'd be going skating about now."

"And tonight we'd go to the midnight service at St. Mark's!" said Liz. "Remember, Mom and Dad, how you can see your breath, walking in from the parking lot?"

We did remember. We wanted every time-hallowed tradition just as it always had been. No changes. Not at Christmastime.

And yet . . . we remembered one very different Christmas. A Christmas when we'd learned something important about change—whenever it comes. We doubted that

Liz could recall many of the details, since she'd been only six years old. So for her as well as Alan we related the story of our Banana Tree Christmas.

We'd been sent with our three children—Scott, then twelve, Donn, age nine, and six-year-old Liz—on a year-long magazine assignment in Uganda. Except for one elderly German couple who lived a quarter-mile below us on a jungle hillside overlooking Lake Victoria, our neighbors were Baganda people, living in mud and thatch houses. Everyone in the family was reveling in the differentness of Africa.

That is, until December. As the Christmas season drew near we realized that this was the time of year when we treasured continuity, not contrast. In his own way, each of us began to mourn. We became positively maudlin about family customs, lamenting that here on the equator we could never hang our stockings by the chimney with care . . . there were no chimneys.

Above all, how could we have Christmas with no Christmas tree—that beautiful evergreen symbol of the undying Life which came to earth at Bethlehem? Stringing the lights, hanging the stars, setting the Herald Angel on the topmost branch . . . every stage of this joyous family activity had pointed to the coming of God's Son. But of course evergreen trees do not grow in the tropics.

At least . . .

One sweltering afternoon in mid-December we looked down the red-earth road that led up through the banana grove and saw the children returning from school. Seventy years of British rule had left behind not only the

English language, but the British school uniform. The boys were dressed in white shirts and very-short khaki pants, Liz in a green dress and gray bowler hat. But . . . what on earth was Scott carrying! Over his left shoulder was what looked for all the world like a freshly cut hemlock.

Faces bright with achievement, the children stopped in our front yard. "Don't look!" Liz called, seeing us in the doorway. While we closed our eyes Scott stood the tree on its sappy stump. "Open!" cried Donn, flourishing—yes, it was a machete, the long, heavy-bladed tool, halfway between a knife and an axe, which every Ugandan household boasts. "Mr. Muwanga loaned it to us," he explained, naming a neighbor at the foot of the hill.

"But—the tree!" we finally managed to get out. "Where in the world—"

"There!" Liz pointed, beaming, down the hill toward . . . the German neighbors. Now that we thought of it, didn't they have an evergreen hedge around their property? A painstakingly tended, infinitely fussed-over and well-nigh-impossible accomplishment in this climate, probably the only stand of hemlock for a thousand miles. We closed our eyes again, willing the tree not to be there when we opened them.

But it was, and there was nothing for it but to set out, all five of us, down that red-dirt road to the Hammerscheimers'.

Down through the banana grove we went. The children, thoroughly subdued, trailed behind, the boys lugging the tree between them. Around a bend there it was:

the Hammerscheimers' hedge, a six-foot hemlock screen, trim and manicured and even . . . except for an eighteen-inch stump and a gaping hole in the very center.

We had met the Hammerscheimers only twice, knew only that he had been a railroad engineer under the British and had stayed on in retirement, devoting himself to—we swallowed hard—gardening. Who knew what patience and expense it had taken to keep evergreens alive on the equator?

As we rapped on the front door, Liz began to cry. Mr. Hammerscheimer spoke English with difficulty, his wife not at all, and we spoke no German. But we had no trouble communicating, given the tree, the tears and—when we led the couple to the scene of the crime—the vandalized hedge. The old German put both hands to his head and began to rock back and forth. We were afraid he might actually be having a heart attack there on the spot, but after the first shock his chief concern seemed to be for his age-stooped little wife.

He spoke to her long and earnestly in German, repeatedly drawing the boughs of the adjacent trees together across the gap as though to reassure her that in time the hedge would fill in.

Then he gestured toward the house: several times we caught the word *Tannenbaum*.

When at last he carried the tree inside, both were smiling. They even insisted we come in, too, while Mrs. Hammerscheimer put on strong Kenya coffee and her husband showed us where in their living-room their unexpectedly harvested *Tannenbaum* would stand. When we left, an hour later, we had two new friends.

But of course we still had no Christmas tree. On either side of us, as we climbed back up the hill toward our house, nodded the long, tattered leaves of the banana jungle. These trees do not produce the yellow dessert-banana we know in the States, but a small green fruit that looks like the yellow banana before it ripens. They never change color, however, and never become soft (we kept a bunch in our kitchen for three months waiting for these things to happen).

These are "matoke" bananas: the Baganda machete off the hard green skin and cook the core like potatoes. Our neighbors consumed great quantities of them each day; in what we took to be a grasshopper approach to the future, they'd hack down the entire tree to get at the single hand of bananas, leaving trunk and leaves on the ground to rot. Both sides of the dirt road were strewn with these fallen trees.

"Maybe," Scott ventured, in the tentative tone of a leader whose previous plan has misfired, "we could use one of these for a Christmas tree."

Our hearts weren't in it, but nobody had a better idea, so we dragged one of the floppy-leafed plants into our living room and stood it in a corner. It did not even remotely look like a Christmas tree, but we set about decorating it anyhow. Our traditional ornaments, of course, were packed in a box in our attic on the other side of the world. Nor did cranberries for cranberry chains grow in Uganda. But we tore the leaves from another banana tree into strips, made banana-ring chains and wound them around the pithy yellow trunk. We'd bought some long, dangling, bead earrings from a Masai tribesman; we hung these from the leaves and tucked small gifts in leaf axils.

We stood back to admire the effect. It still didn't look like a Christmas tree, but it was—well . . . festive! What was there, after all, we began asking ourselves, that was so sacrosanct about the evergreen tree? Originally part of a pagan tradition from northern Europe, it had become a Christmas symbol only because Christians looked for, and found, meaning of their own in it.

What if we made a family project, in the week remaining before Christmas, of finding out everything we could about banana trees? Maybe a Christmas message was hiding here too.

Scott came up with the first one. From his science teacher he learned why local people cut down the whole tree to harvest the fruit. "Each banana tree reproduces only once," he told us. "No matter how long it lives, it won't flower again." What a wonderful symbol for the only-begotten Son of God!

"The matoke banana is the staple food of Central Africa," Donn read from a library book. "For some tribes it constitutes the sole food source." Matoke, then, in this part of the world, was what bread was to Palestine . . . and Jesus said, "I am the bread of heaven."

Liz's first grade class was studying the invention of writing. "In olden days banana leaves were used for paper." Then—the great flat leaves of our tree could stand for the Bible, where the Christmas story was preserved.

Questioning our neighbors, we learned that there is no way to increase the banana tree's yield by human effort. The tree requires no pruning, no fertilizing. Its fruit is a gift . . . like Jesus.

By Christmas Eve we'd become excited about our tree as a symbol of the season we were celebrating. And there was more to come. We'd invited the neighborhood children in for a Christmas Eve party; to the pile of brightly wrapped packages which had been growing all week beneath the tree, now were added the Africans' gifts. And each came wrapped, not in paper and ribbon, but in a banana leaf.

"It's traditional," explained our friend Nnasuubi. "The banana leaf says, 'This is for you.'" Once more, a symbol of God's gift of Himself.

But it was the Hammerscheimers who added the best insight of all. They'd brought a platter of Mrs. Hammerscheimer's *pfeffernusse* for the party, and seemed as delighted as the children as we shared the various ways the tree was speaking to us about Jesus.

"Ja, there is more," said Mr. Hammerscheimer. He pointed to the base of the tree. "Where this tree grew, next year comes a new one!" Like the fruit, it occurs without man's aid. But, for the new to be born, our gardener-neighbor pointed out, the old must die.

This was the best of the gifts we received from our banana Christmas tree: not only a symbol of Christ's death and resurrection, but a reminder of what we were learning about laying down the old to make room for the new.

How full of meaning our tree had become—once we stopped trying to shape it to some earlier model. Why do we resist change so strongly? Why do we cling to the way "it used to be"? It's as though *change* automatically meant *diminishment* . . . the taking away of something precious with nothing of equal value supplied to replace it.

But God never runs out of riches. Why not make a lifelong game of looking for Him *in* change itself!

There'd been many of them in our lives since that year in Uganda. Deaths and births. Career changes, moves, new relationships. And each time, following a bout of nostalgia, we'd found His meaning in the altered situation.

"And we'll find it here in Arizona," we told Alan and Liz as we finished the story. That afternoon the four of us squeezed into the cab of their old half-ton truck and headed out into the brown-and-gold desert.

"I wonder," Liz mused, "how a cactus would work as a Christmas tree . . ."

John and Elizabeth

PART SIX

SEEING GOD IN THE VALLEYS

Seeing Him in all that happens.
In the valleys as well as on the
  mountain peaks.
In the beautiful, but in the ugly too.
Seeing God, whatever else we see.
This is the full picture, the sum of
  all the glimpses of His glory.

The Name Plaque
They were just little scraps of wood, glued together.

An Angel Named Maria
The infant was a "vegetable" without human potential.

A Walk in the Woods
Usually the woods spoke of peace. Not this time.

Lee and the Bear
He was sixteen years old when the disaster occurred.

Report from Cuba
It was a surprising place for a foretaste of heaven.

The Blind Seers of Bwama
In a leper colony we met a joyous faith.

Sometimes it's life's negatives that make His truth stand out.

THE NAME PLAQUE

I sat on the edge of the bed as John unpacked from a trip. Out of his suitcase came a necktie, a toilet kit, a bundle of soiled clothes and—a piece of wood?

I picked it up, puzzled: a rectangular block of redwood maybe two inches high, five inches long, rough beneath my fingers, on one side of which had been glued short lengths of a lighter-colored wood. The blonde wood formed no pattern, spelled nothing, didn't even make a pleasing design.

"I admired it on someone's desk," John said, "and he gave it to me."

"I don't get it. What's it for?"

"To look at." He took it from my hand and set it on the dresser.

"I don't get it," I repeated. It was just a few scraps of wood, crudely stuck together. I hoped he wasn't planning to keep it on the dresser beside my Spode china pin dish. I carried the laundry down to the basement and came back upstairs with coffee. From the dresser top the word leapt across the room at me:

Jesus

The seemingly meaningless arrangement of light-colored sticks in fact formed the negative spaces of a name plaque spelling God's full participation in human life.

The plaque is still on our dresser. Sometimes I see the name so clearly I wonder how I could ever miss it; other times I can't see it at all. Then I remember: it's not the raised parts that spell His name, but the hollows and valleys in between . . .

Elizabeth

Seeing God means enlarging our field of vision to include the damaged, the twisted, the hurt. Not looking away from these things, but through them—straight into the face of Jesus . . .

AN ANGEL NAMED MARIA

It began, the sister told me, with a doctor's voice on the telephone:

"There was a baby born here two weeks ago that no one knows what to do with."

He'd gone on to explain that the infant was a "vegetable"—a hydrocephalic without sight or hearing or any human potential. The mother had disappeared from the hospital after seeing it, and the state was chronically short of funds for handicapped children under the age of six.

"It will never live to be six," the doctor's voice had continued hastily. "At the outside, a few months. Meanwhile there is a problem of care . . ."

"Bring the baby here," the sister said. Sister Marie Patrice was the nun in charge of the day nursery which the Sisters of Mercy ran for working mothers in Charlotte, North Carolina. After hanging up the phone, she said, she'd begun to regret her rash invitation. The babies here at the nursery were normal healthy children; the sisters knew nothing about an infant requiring special care.

That afternoon a car pulled into the driveway. The

doctor carried in a bundle, then pulled aside the hospital blanket for the nun to see. For a moment she could make no sense of the two forms before her. Then she realized that one was an enormous head; the other, where a back should have been, was a tumor the size of the head. Stumps hung where there should have been legs and feet. Only the little arms and hands were formed properly.

Sister Patrice stretched out her arms. "Give her to us," she said.

And so another baby joined the nursery—a baby for whom nobody called when the day was over. A "vegetable" was the last thing she made the sisters think of, for she cried constantly as though in pain.

Whenever they picked her up, however, the crying stopped. So the sisters began carrying her with them while they looked after the other babies, holding her while they ate and went to chapel and even while they slept.

Six months came and went. The baby they had baptized "Maria" grew so heavy that the nuns had to pass her more often from one pair of arms to another. But she would not startle at a noise, nor blink when a hand was passed before her eyes. Never once in all those months had she given a hint of awareness.

And then one day as Sister Patrice rocked her in the nursery playroom, the unbelievable happened.

"She smiled!" the sister cried. "Maria smiled at me!"

Sister Patrice was the only one that day to see the smile. But a few days later another nun saw it, and then another, until the whole convent glowed with Maria's smile.

After that the weeks and months sped by as the sisters

discovered first one talent, then another, in the baby that had no potential. They plunked the nursery piano and discovered that Maria had hearing. They placed her hands on the light switch just inside the cottage door and discovered she had enough muscle control to turn it on and off.

One afternoon when she was almost two, she was playing this favorite game of making the room bright and then dark again, when suddenly she turned to stare at the bulb burning in the ceiling. Her lips parted. "Light!" said Maria.

As a first word it could not have been better chosen. For it seemed to the sisters that with it came light from God that the next step in faith was to be removal of the tumor.

The surgeon they consulted was dubious. Without the tumor, he reasoned, all the excess fluid might settle in the head, distending it still further and hastening death.

But the sisters had glimpsed the hope that is stronger than reason. The tumor was removed, and the very reverse of what the doctor feared occurred. Instead of gaining fluid, the head began to drain. Over a period of two years it shrank nine inches until, as Maria herself grew, it looked nearly normal.

They were wonderful years. The sisters bought a tiny wheelchair that Maria herself could roll with her strong arms and hands. They made a swing and a play table and a special seat in the chapel for her.

Most important to Maria, they bought her shoes. As other little girls dream of being ballerinas, Maria dreamed of wearing shoes. She would never walk, but the sisters understood that shoes are for more than mere locomotion. And so they took her back to the surgeon, and on the unformed legs he shaped a place for shoes to fit.

Meanwhile great changes had come to the little cottage on the convent grounds. As word got around that the sisters were sheltering a defective child, another such infant was brought to them. Then another, and another. These children took more time than normal babies. Some, like Maria, had to be held constantly. Some had to be tube fed, some needed oxygen.

The sisters worked around the clock, and still the babies kept coming from all over the state and far beyond: the mongoloid, the microcephalic, the palsied. And to the sisters, God's light had grown blindingly clear. There were other nurseries around Charlotte for normal children. For these injured ones, there was nowhere else.

I'd come to visit Holy Angels Nursery wondering how a home that held only deformed babies would affect me. A curly-haired little girl met me at the door, the ruffles of her starched blue dress concealing the arms of a wheelchair. "I'm very pleased to meet you," she said politely. "Do you like my shoes?"

Of course it was Maria. Her shoes were white, with little bells on them and lace around the top, and I told her truthfully that they were gorgeous. Maria and Sister Patrice led me through the sunny new home built with gifts from Protestants, Jews, and Catholics all over the country. And as we walked from room to room, misgiving gave way to a feeling I could not name. Baby-blue cribs with new toys in them lined walls hung with Mother Goose scenes. Every baby girl wore a pretty dress, every boy a crisp romper, no two alike. Volunteers from a nearby girls' school crooned to babies in rocking chairs around the room. It was like stepping into the private nursery of a treasured only child—multiplied by dozens.

I believe they were each an only child to Sister Patrice as she recounted the life-and-death struggle waged over each crib. "We were so worried about Johnny last week, but penicillin is helping." "The doctors don't give George another month. But," squeezing the tiny hand, "we're going to fool them, aren't we, George?"

On we went, crib after crib—sixty-seven of them—and in each one, the sister's favorite child. I saw babies from Jewish families and Christian ones, blacks and whites, children of architects and mill hands, doctors and migrant workers. The only thing I didn't see was a second-hand toy or a threadbare blanket. "Most of them can't see, you know," said the sister. "That's why it's up to us to be sure they have only pretty things."

We reached the last room, and I realized what it was I had been feeling. In each crib Sister Patrice had made me see a person, an individual unique in all creation, a human soul of infinite worth. When I told her so, she beamed.

"Oh, yes!" she said. "And do you know what the greatest moment of all is? When this person leaps free at last from his poor, hurt body!"

She had been at the cribside each time a baby died, she

said. "God tells me when He is taking one of them. And then this little person stands suddenly free, whole and straight. It's only an instant, you know, for these babies fly straight to the heart of God."

I stared at the sister, at the bottles of blood plasma behind her, the oxygen tents, the rows of drugs. I hardly knew how to phrase the question that was in my mind.

"Why struggle then to keep them here as long as we can?" she asked for me. She ran her hand through the gold-brown curls that make a halo of Maria's head.

"God has all the bright angels of heaven for His joy," she said gently. "We struggling servants of His here below—we need angels too."

Elizabeth

What can nature teach us about loss?

A WALK IN THE WOODS

I went outside, after the bad news came, and took my usual path through the woods. Not headed anywhere: too stunned to pray or even to cry. Someone dear to me had died, needlessly, senselessly, and the shock was like a physical blow.

Always before, in times of stress, the woods had spoken to me of a world of beauty and serenity, far removed from the ugliness we men create. That morning, however, no such comfort came.

On the contrary, the peace of the woods seemed an affront to the cruel realities of life. The fluttering leaves, the silly, chirping birds, were irrelevant to the pain I felt. I glanced up through the branches at the blue, uncaring sky—and stopped short.

Above my head the trunk of the tree was split in two. One of the halves ended in a jagged stump, perhaps the result of a long-ago lightning strike, while new growth from the surviving half stretched to fill the empty space.

Slowly I walked on. A few yards farther the heart of a chestnut oak was eaten away with disease, a thin outer layer soaring skyward around a hollow core. Here insects had left a gall wound, there a branch was missing. Everywhere I looked were signs of trauma and loss.

But . . . all these were living trees: drawing life from the sun, giving it back as food, oxygen, shelter.

It was far from the time when my own wound would grow a protective shell. Farther still until I could turn my healing into help for others. But what I'd seen that morning was loss and gain, not as opposites, but as the seamless fabric of God's natural world.

Elizabeth

God speaks through all of nature. But in the great wildernesses His voice is especially clear . . .

LEE AND THE BEAR

This is a story about a sixteen-year-old Alaskan. I think it says something about wilderness that city people like me need to know. Perhaps it's simply that God looks different out-of-doors. Perhaps indoors we loom too large, whittling away at God to fit Him into our man-sized structures.

John and Lee Hagmeier were twins, though being born was about the last thing the two boys did together. John was the gregarious type, loved Juneau with its people and excitement. Lee was happiest in the forests outside of town. But Lee took a job in town, that summer of 1959, stocking shelves at a supermarket. Lee planned to be a conservationist and he needed money for college.

July 27 was a Monday, Lee's day off. He and his friend Doug Dobbins went fishing up Montana Creek, several miles above the saw mill. They were far upstream when they began to see bear signs: a half-eaten fish on the bank, the shallow bed that a bear hollows out at the foot of a tree. Lee shifted his heavy bear gun from shoulder to shoulder. The boys were not overly concerned about black bear, which are common outside Juneau. But the brown bear was something else: three times larger than the blackie, fast and ferocious. Usually the brown bear stays in the mountains. But 1959 was a poor blueberry summer; brownies had been reported foraging at lower altitudes.

It happened when Lee and Doug were crossing an alder thicket. The bear charged without warning. Doug, who had no gun, saw him first.

"Lee," he shouted. "A brownie!"

With one motion Lee swung his gun from his shoulder and released the safety. But the bear reached him first. Lee went down on his back and his shot went wild. The bear sank his teeth through Lee's thick waders and into his right knee. Lifting him by the leg, he shook him as a dog shakes a rat. Then he let go and Lee dropped to the ground.

Lee lay still, his eyes closed, knowing that the slightest motion could bring another attack. Just as Lee began to think the animal had wandered away, he felt the bear's teeth on both sides of his face, just at eye level. He moaned once as the bear's jaws closed.

In the thick brush, Doug could not see what had happened. He heard Lee's shot, a sound of scuffling, then the bear ran past him and went crashing away through the trees.

"Lee!" Doug shouted. "Lee, are you all right?"

There was silence. Then Lee's voice: "No, I'm not all right, Doug," he said. "Don't be shocked when you see me."

Doug tore through the bushes, stared, then closed his eyes. The shock was that Lee could still be alive and talking to him. The top of his face appeared to be ripped away. Doug picked up the gun and fired three shots into the air, the hunter's traditional call for help. Neither boy really believed there was anyone within hearing; in the back of both minds was the bear. Bears have a way of returning to the scene of a mauling.

"Lee," asked Doug, "could you stand if I held you?"

Panting and struggling, he got Lee to his feet, but Lee's knee would not support him. Doug knew he could never carry Lee out alone. He pulled him to a tree, administered what first aid he could, then propped him into a sitting position. "I'm going for help," he said. He thought of the lonesome country that lay between them and the saw mill.

"It'll be a while, Lee," he said. "Hold on!"

The bear had headed east so Doug went west, gashing a tree with his knife every few steps to mark the way back. At the creek he stuck the knife into a tree to mark the spot and then started downstream, now running, now crawling on hands and knees through the choking brush. An hour later his breath was short, his heart a great lump of pain.

He was still a long way from the mill when he stumbled on two of the loggers working deep in the woods. One of the men went with Doug, the other ran back to the mill.

Back in the alder thicket, in a world suddenly night-black, Lee waited. He was not conscious of fainting, but it seemed to him that Doug was back almost at once. Doug and the logger lifted him between them and started the long carry out of the forest.

Halfway out they were met by six men and a stretcher from the mill. At the road an ambulance was waiting and at the hospital in Juneau, Dr. C. C. Carter, who had delivered the Hagmeier twins sixteen years before.

Dr. Carter held out to Lee's parents only one chance in fifty that Lee would live. To nurses at the hospital he added that it would take a miracle to bring that one chance about.

But the miracle happened.

When I went to interview Lee there in the hospital, it was with a sense of dread. How do you talk to a sixteen-year-old outdoorsman who has lost his eyes?

I rehearsed a few cheerful words: how nice that the people of Juneau had started a fund for him; what wonders plastic surgeons achieve these days. The words sounded hollow even to me.

I left his hospital room in a totally different mood: I had with me the unforgettable memory of a smile.

His smile was about all of Lee's face I could see: the rest was wrapped in bandages. But it was a terrific smile. Doug was with him and with much interrupting and correcting of each other they told me the story I have just related.

With growing amazement I listened as they quarreled and joked about the events of that day as matter-of-factly as though Lee had got the bear, instead of the other way around.

Lee felt for some phonograph records he had been given. "They've got whole books on records today," he told me eagerly. "But of course I'm going to learn Braille too. Lots of colleges accept you if you can read Braille."

I stared at him. I could think of nothing to say.

So it was Lee who talked, intently and earnestly, about conservation, about fish and game management, about laws to protect wildlife. "The right laws are the first thing. If you could say that in your magazine—"

As Lee continued his plea for the beauty he would never see again, I was haunted with the feeling that he was leaving something unsaid.

Suddenly I knew what it was. I have interviewed many people in the aftermath of disaster, and a single theme invariably runs through their accounts. The theme is: "Why? Why did it happen? Why me?"

Lee Hagmeier was not asking why. As simply and un-questioningly as a tree falls in the forest, he accepted this thing that had occurred.

Lee did go on to school, and to work as a conservation lawyer. As simply as a tree . . . perhaps that is Lee's secret. In God's natural world there is no "Why me?" Animals are born and die, the wind blows or the sun shines. There is no protest, only a vast "Praise be to God." Perhaps this is the wisdom which fishermen and mountain climbers and all who live intimately with nature take away from her great silences.

Elizabeth

*Christians under Communism . . . this is the valley
in which millions in our century have found themselves.
In 1987 Elizabeth filed this . . .*

REPORT FROM CUBA

As the gray-green sugar cane fields spread beneath our plane, the couple beside me turned away from the window. "What if we're not allowed beyond Havana?" Vera asked.

After twenty-seven years Vera and her husband, Paul, were returning to the country where they'd gone as newlywed missionaries. For seven years the couple had worked in Cuba's feudal interior, where fifty percent of the population could not read, where a lucky cane cutter found work half the time. We hoped to be able to get to their small inland city to see if the church they had started was still there.

When they'd invited me to come with them, I'd jumped at the chance. I too remembered Cuba before the revolution—very different memories. My brother had worked in Havana for General Electric. To me, Cuba meant warm beaches, Latin music; for the tourist, Cuba had been heaven on earth.

Havana airport was below us now, reassuringly familiar: the low, whitewashed terminal building and small control tower just as I remembered them. But as our plane bumped to a halt and a crew pushed forward a stairway on wheels, I realized there was nothing reassuring about an airport that had not changed in three decades . . .

Since scheduled airlines no longer fly between the United States and Cuba, we had booked ourselves on an eight-day tour from Mexico City. After customs formalities, a pretty young Cuban woman ushered our group—mostly Mexican vacationers—aboard a bus into the city, pointing out along the way the new hospitals that have made Cuba a pacesetter in public medicine. I stared out the window, grateful for whatever holiday was keeping the traffic off the streets. I recalled this drive from the airport as a sped-up movie of careening cars and honking horns.

The lobby of our hotel had been refurbished in Cuba's current bid for tourism. Upstairs in my room, however, the rug was stained, the paper peeling. Recalling those lively Cuban dance bands, I switched on the black-and-white Russian-made TV. On the screen two men faced each other across a table; they were so motionless I thought at first it was a still picture. Then I realized it was a game of chess—Cuba with a Russian accent.

While Paul tried to arrange a trip inland, I was adjusting to a country strangely subdued. It wasn't a holiday, for example, that had emptied the streets, but the high cost of gasoline. What traffic there was, furthermore, proceeded in a most un-Cuban fashion, stopping at lights, obeying speed limits.

I took a taxi through these sedate avenues to my brother's former apartment building—now, like the rest of the city, badly in need of paint. On the way we passed an extraordinary fortress-like structure topped by a high tower. The new Russian embassy, the taxi driver informed me. "It's . . . ah, very striking," I ventured.

"Very ugly," he corrected me. What was worse, he went on, the Russians had brought their own workmen to build it. But he spoke without emotion. In the Cuba I remembered, a taxi driver relating such an insult would have taken both hands off the wheel and left the driving to chance as he made his point.

To our relief, there was only minor awkwardness about leaving the tour for three days. Paul had managed to rent a Russian-made car, a small gray Lada, enabling us to visit a number of towns en route to their former church. At each stop, we had a name, an address. Our procedure was always to park the Lada at some neutral spot and walk to our destination, not because of any risk to us, but because Cuban Christians bear the crushing charge of being unpatriotic. To have foreigners park at their doorways could only fuel neighbors' suspicions.

Especially foreigners from the United States. The Bay of Pigs invasion is replayed endlessly—on radio and TV, on highway billboards: *Beware the aggressor to the north!*

"We are watched all the time," one pastor told us as we sat in his tiny storefront church, halfway to the town where Vera and Paul had worked. "Everyone who attends service is reported to the authorities."

What happens then? Nothing particular. Perhaps a friendly visit from a local official to warn of possible consequences at work. Good jobs go to good citizens; to attend church means to abandon ambition.

The price has at times been higher. Though the Cuban constitution, on paper, guarantees freedom of religion, the number of Christians jailed, tortured and executed "for treason" is far greater than statistically probable. Every congregation we visited could recall episodes of harassment. "The police locked the outside door one Sunday," a Catholic priest recalled. "Kept us there until four o'clock the next morning."

A woman in another church described how militiamen burst into a service, snatched her Bible from her hands, threw it to the floor and trampled it.

But these are memories from the 1960s when counter-revolutionary fears were high. Today Christians are not so much persecuted as looked down on, considered less than loyal. For Cubans, so in love with their beautiful island, this is a terrible price all by itself. Add the economic hardships, and it is clear that Christians have reason to seek a new life elsewhere, as so many Cubans have done.

But the Christians we were meeting had stayed. Why?

Here is one man's answer. Thirty miles from the town where Paul and Vera's church had once been located, we found Juan's small house. When Juan first met Paul and Vera at an outdoor youth rally thirty-three years ago, he was an eighteen-year-old about to enter engineering school.

"I heard God calling me to the ministry at that rally," Juan told us. "But I bargained with Him. I told Him if

He'd help me get my engineering degree, I'd go to seminary afterward and pastor part-time."

Juan kept his promise. He landed a top job with an engineering firm and at the same time developed a night-time rescue mission among the prostitutes of Santiago de Cuba. Then came the revolution. Juan's Christian commitment was too profound for him to deny it, as some at his firm did. He was demoted from his management position and placed under one of his own trainees. Recognizing that there was no future for him in Cuba, he and his wife applied to leave the country.

For that, Juan was dismissed from his job altogether and sent to work in the sugar fields, where he earned barely enough to support a family that now included four children. As would-be emigrants they were denied ration cards and became dependent on the charity of friends for even such basics as bread and cooking fuel.

It was two years before the precious exit visa was granted. The family of six took the long bus trip to Havana. Their luggage was actually aboard the plane when an official spotted the word "engineer" in Juan's papers. "Engineers are not permitted to emigrate."

In vain, Juan pointed out that he had not been allowed to work as an engineer for two years. The visa was withdrawn, and the family returned to Santiago de Cuba to find that their house had already been assigned to others. For two more years friends helped out as he pursued his efforts to leave.

"And then one day," he said, "I realized Who was behind all the frustration. It wasn't the officials—they were only His tools. God Himself was reminding me, 'I called you to minister to My people.'"

Juan withdrew his application to emigrate. His citizen status was restored, an engineering post offered him. But this time Juan followed the Voice he had heard so many years before. He became a full-time pastor, serving half a dozen small congregations. Juan cannot hope for the crowds he remembers from his teens; outdoor religious meetings, for example, are outlawed. But membership in his churches is slowly growing, and he ministers to others in secret. Why does he stay in Cuba? "God wants me here."

Our final destination was an hour away. As we drew near, tension in the car mounted. How often Paul and Vera had talked about the church they'd started in an abandoned bakery building. About Tomas, who could not read, memorizing every word of every hymn. About young Alicia and Pedro, who met at an evening service, later married, then promised to pastor the church when the Americans were forced to leave.

"That was long ago," Paul and Vera kept reminding each other now. "Who knows if they stayed? If anyone stayed?"

Again we parked the Lada and set out on foot. At the converted bakery, Paul knocked at a side door leading to the three-room parsonage he and Vera had carved from a corner of the building.

The door was opened by a gray-haired woman who stared at the three foreigners in surprise, then beckoned us quickly inside. In the dim interior she stared from face to face.

". . . Alicia?" Vera asked.

". . . Vera?"

Then the two women were in each other's arms. A tall, balding man appeared from another room: Pedro. Eleven family members were currently living in those three small rooms. Was housing so scarce here? Well, you know: a pastor is an "unproductive" member of society, low on waiting lists . . .

Chairs were crowded into the small living room-kitchen as word spread and the street door admitted new arrivals. Again and again I watched the same drama repeated. A middle-aged man or woman staring at Paul, then at Vera. A gasp of recognition. A long embrace.

I talked to Tomas. The man who used to memorize hymns because he could not read, now writes them. (Cuba today has 96 percent literacy.) Like so many Christians, Tomas had been in prison. "God wanted me there," he told me, echoing words we had heard from Juan.

How could he say that? Why, because evangelism is outlawed. Christians are not permitted to travel about preaching. But in the prison barracks were men from all over the island. Today five thriving house churches date from Tomas's time behind bars.

We were taken into the sanctuary. The church, about whose survival Paul and Vera had wondered all these years, had been enlarged by six additional rows since their time. Behind the altar the baptismal tank was so new the plaster was still damp. They'd hurried it through so that fourteen people could be baptized the previous Sunday—and that was only those willing to make their new commitment public.

The door continued to open and shut, admitting people carrying food—a loaf of bread, a handful of eggs. An enormous meal was being prepared for the visitors. Rice, beans, yucca, potatoes, chicken. I stared at the helpings pressed upon me, knowing that every one of these items was rationed. How many coupons had it taken to buy this much?

Everyone joined in the grace: those few who could squeeze beside us at the small table, the thirty who stood around the walls, thanking God for food and faith. For love among Christians of "enemy" nations. For eyes to discern God's will and strength to do it. "For placing us in heaven," as Tomas put it, "here on earth."

Heaven on earth . . . Those were the words that echoed in my heart as the plane lifted off two days later from old-fashioned Havana airport. I'd spent a week among people who lived with government repression and neighbors' scorn. But if heaven is where God's will is recognized and done, then for the past eight days that's where I'd been.

Elizabeth

Seeing God does not depend on physical sight...

THE BLIND SEERS OF BWAMA

We were halfway across the lake when the drums began. They had an eerie, compelling quality there in the heart of tropical Africa: the jungle returned the sounds muted and mysterious. We were on our way to Bwama Island, a leper colony in the middle of Lake Bunyonyi in western Uganda, not far from the Congo border.

Dr. Robert Parry, medical director of the colony, leaned closer and spoke over the roar of the outboard motor. "Eighty years ago," he said, "those drums were the most dreaded sound in the whole district."

In those days Bwama Island was the stronghold of witch doctors, who held the area with chains of fear. At full moon people on the mainland could expect to hear the drums on Bwama. It was the signal for tribute. Villagers around the lake would hurry to their dugout canoes with fruit, vegetables, chickens, a few young girls—all to be left by night on the shore of the island. Any village which failed to obey the summons of the drums was cursed.

When the British government finally drove the witch doctors away, no one would live on Bwama Island. Then, in the early 1920s, English medical missionaries arrived in western Uganda to set up the first hospitals in this region.

Needing a separate center for the thousands of leprosy sufferers, the missionaries took over the witch doctors' island. Here they saw a chance to demonstrate to the superstitious tribesmen that the God they served was more powerful than the evil spirits of the magicians.

With this in mind, the first structure they built on the island was not the leprosarium but the church. It was from the porch of this church that the drums were now thundering. Only now, the call was not for tribute but for prayer.

We landed at a tiny dock and took a narrow footpath through dense vegetation. The first few houses we passed, round mud-and-grass affairs like most buildings in this part of Africa, were empty—testimony to the new sulfa drugs which in the past ten years had reduced the number of patients from 850 to 250.

We moved out of the thick growth and onto cultivated fields. Beyond was a grove of banana trees and beyond that, more houses. Insofar as possible, Bwama patients are encouraged to maintain normal living habits, to set up housekeeping, grow their own food and keep their children near them at the special Healthy Children's House on the island.

"Let's meet some of our permanent boarders."

Dr. Parry spoke as though he were offering us a great privilege, but it was the moment Tib and I had been dreading. These were the people who, though their disease had been arrested, would never leave the island. The destruction of their bodies had gone too far; they were incapable of caring for themselves.

On the far side of the banana grove we found ourselves in a compound full of people. Many were lying on the ground, others walking about with a curious stumbling gait, none paying the least attention to us. It was a full moment before we realized that all of them were blind.

Dr. Parry led us forward, speaking to each person by name. He stopped before a barrel-chested man lying on the ground. "This is Amos," said Dr. Parry. "He's been especially eager to meet you."

I looked down. The man's hands and feet were stumps, his eyes milk white. But he was powerfully built, perhaps still young. He was speaking with great earnestness in the native tongue.

"He asks you to take a message to America," said Dr. Parry. "Tell the Americans that we suffer in our bodies, but that in our hearts we rejoice!"

I stared incredulously at the man lying in the African sun. "Why?" I asked. "Why does he rejoice?"

Dr. Parry obtained the answer from Amos. "He says he rejoices because God loves him."

I swallowed hard. "The message will be passed on," I assured him.

Our next stop was at the door of a mud-and-wattle hut. Inside, a bent old woman sat on the foot of a bed where an even older and more twisted man was lying. Both were blind.

"Martha came here to visit with her old friend John," said Dr. Parry. "I shall introduce you." We heard the words *America* and *Guideposts*. Martha turned her head toward us.

"We can't see you with our eyes," Dr. Parry translated for her. "But we can see you with our hearts. We welcome you in the name of the Lord Jesus."

The old man lifted a fingerless hand. "We can't see you now," he corrected her, chuckling at having caught her on a theological point. "But in Heaven we will meet face to face."

We walked on through the compound, seeing something that at first the misshaped bodies had concealed from us: these people were happy. Everywhere we were greeted with smiles, shouts of joy, words of welcome.

"You see," Dr. Parry said, "these people come from a world far more terrible than the one you see here. Ninety-five percent of them arrive in Bwama as pagans, animists, people for whom the reality behind the world is evil. They've spent their lives trying to ward off the innumerable curses which they believed it was the will of the universe to inflict on them.

"Here, for the first time, they hear that reality is not like that. They hear that God is love, that their hurt is His hurt. They don't have to take our word for it. They feel the gentle hands of the nurses. They taste warm food. They lie on real beds, out of the rain. They've been down to the deepest pit, these people, and there in the abyss they've found the Everlasting Arms."

Seeing God in the valleys . . . perhaps those who've known the world without Him, see Him best. Perhaps in the darkness He shines brightest of all.

John